Making Integration Work

Young People with Migrant Parents

OECD

This work is published under the responsibility of the Secretary-General of the OECD. The opinions expressed and arguments employed herein do not necessarily reflect the official views of OECD member countries.

This document, as well as any data and map included herein, are without prejudice to the status of or sovereignty over any territory, to the delimitation of international frontiers and boundaries and to the name of any territory, city or area.

The statistical data for Israel are supplied by and under the responsibility of the relevant Israeli authorities. The use of such data by the OECD is without prejudice to the status of the Golan Heights, East Jerusalem and Israeli settlements in the West Bank under the terms of international law.

Note by Turkey
The information in this document with reference to "Cyprus" relates to the southern part of the Island. There is no single authority representing both Turkish and Greek Cypriot people on the Island. Turkey recognises the Turkish Republic of Northern Cyprus (TRNC). Until a lasting and equitable solution is found within the context of the United Nations, Turkey shall preserve its position concerning the "Cyprus issue".

Note by all the European Union Member States of the OECD and the European Union
The Republic of Cyprus is recognised by all members of the United Nations with the exception of Turkey. The information in this document relates to the area under the effective control of the Government of the Republic of Cyprus.

Please cite this publication as:
OECD (2021), *Young People with Migrant Parents*, Making Integration Work, OECD Publishing, Paris, *https://doi.org/10.1787/6e773bfe-en*.

ISBN 978-92-64-79116-9 (print)
ISBN 978-92-64-94156-4 (pdf)

Making Integration Work
ISSN 2522-7718 (print)
ISSN 2522-7726 (online)

Foreword

This is the fourth publication in "Making Integration Work", a series that summarises main lessons from the OECD's work on integration policies. The objective is to present in a non-technical way the main challenges and good policy practices to support the lasting integration of immigrants and their children.

This fourth edition takes stock of the experiences of OECD countries in the integration of young people with migrant parents. It summarises this along 11 main policy lessons with supporting examples of good practice. It also provides a comprehensive comparison of the policy frameworks that govern policy strategies for the integration of young people with migrant parents in OECD countries. Information about the different policy frameworks was gathered through a questionnaire.

Previous editions of this series addressed the integration of refugees and others in need of protection, the assessment and recognition of foreign qualifications and the integration of family migrants. A further booklet will cover language training for adult migrants.

Acknowledgements

This booklet was written by Anne-Sophie Senner and Karolin Krause (both Consultants to the OECD), together with Elisabeth Kamm (OECD) under the co-ordination of Thomas Liebig from the OECD's International Migration Division. The OECD Secretariat developed this booklet with financial support from Stiftung Mercator (Germany) through the Maecenata Foundation. It also benefitted from seed money for the series "Making Integration Work" through grants from Germany (the Federal Ministry for Family Affairs, Senior Citizens, Women and Youth), Norway (the Ministry of Education and Research), Sweden (the Ministry of Employment) and the King Baudouin Foundation (Belgium). This work would not have been possible without the support of the delegates to the OECD's Working Party on Migration and the national authorities in charge of integration and youth policies, who willingly shared their knowledge of national policy frameworks and programmes.

Table of contents

Foreword   3

Acknowledgements   4

Introduction   8
    Why is the integration of young people with migrant parents an important issue?   8
    Young people with migrant parents face challenges in the education system …   9
    … and in the labour market   9
    The purpose of this publication   10

1. Use inclusive language to refer to youth with migrant parents   11
    WHAT and WHY?   11
    WHO?   11
    HOW?   12

2. Make sure all children start school on an equal footing   14
    WHAT and WHY?   14
    WHO?   14
    HOW?   15

3. Provide flexible education pathways for youth born abroad   23
    WHAT and WHY?   23
    WHO?   23
    HOW?   24

4. Involve immigrant parents in the education process   32
    WHAT and WHY?   32
    WHO?   32
    HOW?   32

5. Reduce the concentration of disadvantaged youth with immigrant parents   36
    WHAT and WHY?   36
    WHO?   36
    HOW?   37

6. Prevent school drop-out and establish second-chance programmes   45
    WHAT and WHY?   45
    WHO?   45

HOW?   46

7. Promote educational excellence and role modelling   51
    WHAT and WHY?   51
    WHO?   51
    HOW?   52

8. Facilitate the school-to-work transition   56
    WHAT and WHY?   56
    WHO?   56
    HOW?   57

9. Tackle discrimination and encourage diversity   60
    WHAT and WHY?   60
    WHO?   60
    HOW?   61

10. Foster social integration through sports and associations   65
    WHAT and WHY?   65
    WHO?   65
    HOW?   66

11. Encourage naturalisation   68
    WHAT and WHY?   68
    WHO?   68
    HOW?   68
    References   73

FIGURES

Figure 1. Foreign-born and native-born youth with migrant parents in OECD countries, 2017   8
Figure 2.1. Early Childhood Education and Care (ECEC) attendance rates, by place of birth of parents or
guardians   15
Figure 5.1. How different factors affect academic performance   37
Figure 6.1. Early school leavers   46
Figure 7.1. Highly educated by parents' place of birth   52
Figure 8.1. Percentage of youth aged 15-34 who are not in employment, education or training (NEET), 2017   57
Figure 9.1. Self-reported discrimination   61

TABLES

Table 2.1. Early language screening and stimulation   18
Table 2.2. Early Childhood Education and Care   20
Table 2.3. Free access to Early Childhood Education and Care, 2016 or latest available year   21
Table 3.1. Specific reception classes for recently arrived youth in OECD countries, 2016   26
Table 3.2. Targeted support offers for late arrivals in OECD countries, 2016   28
Table 3.3. Training of origin country languages at school in OECD countries, 2017 or latest available year   30
Table 4.1. Initiatives to involve immigrant parents in their children's education in OECD countries, 2016   34
Table 5.1. Additional funding for schools with disadvantaged students in OECD countries, 2016   39
Table 5.2. Allocation of additional teaching staff in the mainstream classroom and incentives for teachers to
work in schools with disadvantaged students in OECD countries, 2016   42

Table 6.1. VET bridging programmes and second chance offers for school drop-outs, including young people with migrant parents in OECD countries, 2016   48

Table 7.1. Policies to promote participation of young people with migrant parents in the public sector in OECD countries, 2016   54

Table 9.1. Measures to tackle discriminatory hiring practices against young people with migrant parents in OECD countries, 2016   63

Table 11.1. National legislation on the acquisition of citizenship at birth for children of immigrants and legal framework with respect to dual citizenship, 2018   70

Table 11.2. Legal framework with respect to the conditions for the acquisition of citizenship through naturalisation in OECD countries, 2018   71

Follow OECD Publications on:

http://twitter.com/OECD_Pubs

http://www.facebook.com/OECDPublications

http://www.linkedin.com/groups/OECD-Publications-4645871

http://www.youtube.com/oecdilibrary

http://www.oecd.org/oecddirect/

Introduction

Why is the integration of young people with migrant parents an important issue?

OECD-wide, youth who are either themselves foreign-born or who are native-born with foreign-born parents account for nearly one in five 15 to 34-year-olds, or 38.7 million people (OECD/EU, 2018[1]). Their population share is increasing in virtually all OECD countries, although the size and composition varies greatly across countries, reflecting countries' different migration histories. Irrespective of whether they migrated or not, some of these young people hold the citizenship of their country of residence, while others do not. In this publication, the term "youth with migrant parents" refers to all youth who are migrants (foreign-born) themselves but arrived during childhood, as well as those who are native-born but have at least one parent who is foreign-born.

Figure 1. Foreign-born and native-born youth with migrant parents in OECD countries, 2017

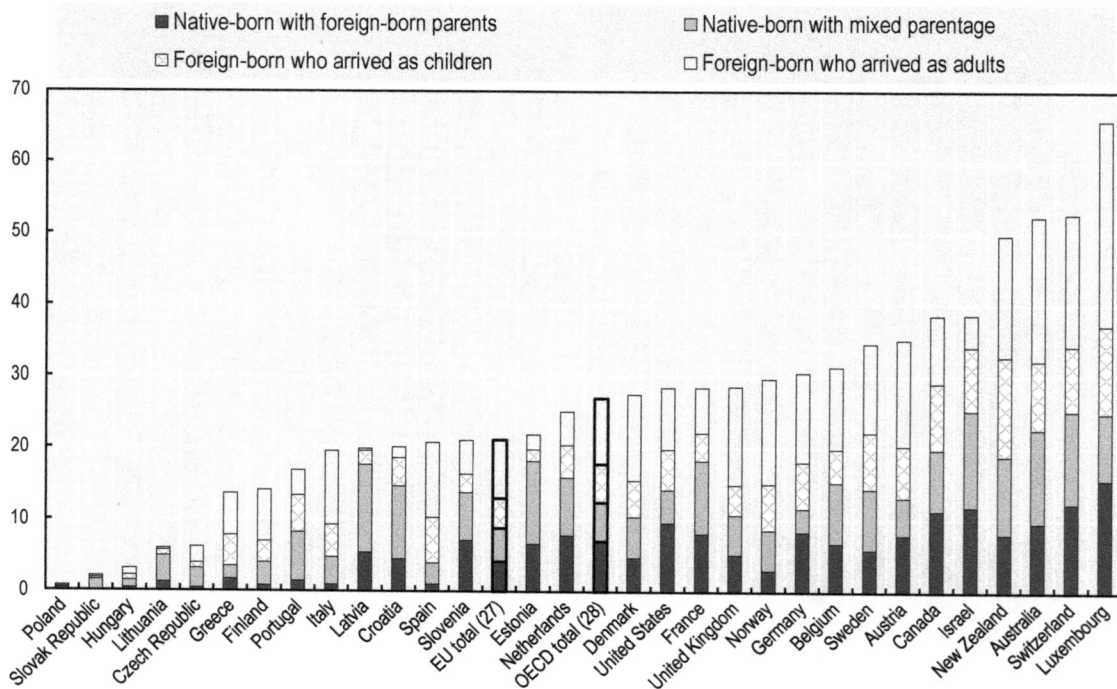

Note: In Germany, the parental origin is based on the country of birth of parents for the native-born still living with their parents, and on own citizenship or the citizenship at birth of the parents for those who do not live anymore with their parents. Averages factor in rates that cannot be published individually because sample sizes are too small.
Source: OECD/EU (2018[1]).

While immigrants who arrived as adults will always face some challenges related to the fact that they have been raised and educated in a different country and education system – and often language – this should not be the case for youth who arrived with their parents as children, and certainly not for youth who have foreign-born parents but are themselves native-born. As a result, they are generally considered the benchmark for successful integration policies.

Young people with migrant parents face challenges in the education system …

Youth with migrant parents often face specific challenges in the education system. Data from the OECD Programme of International Student Assessment (PISA) show that in all OECD countries with the exception of New Zealand, foreign-born students have lower educational outcomes at age 15 (OECD/EU, 2018[1]). The situation for those who are native-born with immigrant parents is more diverse. In OECD Europe, they lag behind their peers with native-born parents by over half a school year. The gap exceeds one year of schooling in the Nordic countries and in longstanding immigrant destinations such as Austria, Belgium, France, Germany, the Netherlands and Switzerland. In contrast, in Australia, Canada and New Zealand, which have disproportionately large shares of high-educated immigrants, native-born students with foreign-born parents have higher educational outcomes than their peers with native-born parents.

Adjusting to a language of instruction that is different from their first language is a major challenge for many young people with migrant parents, especially for those who are foreign-born. In addition, immigrant parents, despite good intentions and in many cases high ambitions, are often less able than native-born parents to support their child's learning in school. The reasons are manifold and include a mix of language difficulties, lack of familiarity with the host country's education system and low awareness of available support offers, sometimes exacerbated by a lack of financial means to invest in remedial learning offers.

Foreign-born students who have spent several years in an education system abroad with a different curriculum and teaching methods face additional hurdles. In addition to language barriers, 'late arrivals' need to adapt to a new learning environment, which is particularly difficult for those who come from lower-performing education systems. PISA results suggest that the older a child is at the time of arrival, the less likely it is to attain baseline levels of academic proficiency at age 15 in math, reading and sciences (OECD, 2018[2]).

Children of immigrants who successfully complete secondary education often struggle to enter further education pathways. Compared with their peers of native-born parentage they are less likely to find an apprenticeship, although this type of training tends to be of particular benefit for children of immigrants (OECD, 2017[3]). At the same time, and despite high educational aspirations, children of immigrants are underrepresented in higher education, which is an important factor for occupational mobility and good labour market performance.

… and in the labour market

Entering the labour market constitutes a challenge for many youth. Lower performance and reading levels put students with migrant parents at an over-proportionate risk of leaving school early and of facing subsequent unemployment. OECD-wide, 14% of the 15-34 year-old native-born children of immigrants are not in employment, education or training (NEET) and in two-thirds of OECD-countries, native-born with foreign-born parents are more likely than their peers with native parentage to be both NEET and low-educated (OECD/EU, 2018[1]).

Compared with their peers of native-born parentage, offspring of immigrants also need more time, on average, to find their first job after finishing school (OECD/EU, 2015[4]). Youth with migrant parents can often rely on fewer social networks to help them obtain relevant information and improve their opportunities in the job-search process. They often lack role models to look up to and remain underrepresented in the public sector in a number of OECD countries. Negative stereotypes and discrimination are further components that complicate both, the search for a first job and subsequent career advancement. Those who have obtained their qualifications abroad often face further challenges related to the assessment and recognition of their credentials.

The purpose of this publication

Ensuring that youth with migrant parents can reach their full potential, in the education system and in the labour market, is both an economic imperative and key to social cohesion. There is a balance to strike between providing mainstream programmes for all youth in need of support, and designing programmes that account for the particular needs of youth with migrant parents. Building on 14 countries reviews on the integration of immigrants and their children and further comparative work by the OECD (OECD, 2010[5]; OECD, 2017[3]; OECD, 2018[6]), this publication presents key lessons and examples of good practice from OECD countries, to highlight ways in which policy-makers can tackle key barriers and support integration.

1. Use inclusive language to refer to youth with migrant parents

WHAT and WHY?

Language reflects and influences attitudes, behaviours and perceptions. Using inclusive language to refer to individuals and groups is thus essential for social cohesion. Against this background, referring inclusively to migrants and their children is no easy task, but one that receives increased attention.

The term 'youth with migrant parents' in this publication includes both native-born youth with migrant parents and foreign-born youth. It also includes native-born youth for whom just one parent immigrated. This definition, as well as the usage and scope of the term, is not universal. Some OECD countries speak of 'migrant generations' and others refer to this group as 'youth with a migrant background'. Some OECD countries exclude youth with one native- and one foreign-born parent, while others even include native-born youth whose parents are native-born but whose grandparents migrated, especially in countries where offspring of immigrants have limited or delayed access to citizenship (Will, 2019[7]). In OECD countries that were settled by migration, native-born youth with migrant parents are rarely in the focus – indeed their outcomes are often above those of their peers with native-born parents (OECD/EU, 2018[1]).

In statistics as well as in daily life, the term 'migration background' can be self-ascribed or ascribed by others. Self-identification, as well as the labels others choose, can impact individuals' integration, including feelings of belonging, attitudes and experiences (Portes and Rumbaut, 2001[8]). Identification and self-labelling often depends on context. In a recent study from Sweden, youth with migrant parents, born or growing up in Sweden, self-identified differently in school, their neighbourhood and abroad, with respect to their nationality (Swedish, Swedish-hyphenated) or ethnic affiliation (Behtoui, 2019[9]). Further, in different countries and languages, different terms are more socially acceptable than others.

The most appropriate term for youth with migrant parents is likewise context dependant. For example, referring to native-born youth with migrant parents as 'children of immigrants' can be factually correct, but might not be appropriate for those who are adults. Speaking of a 'host-country' can be relevant when talking about individuals who recently migrated, but is not appropriate for youth raised and educated in that country.

WHO?

OECD-wide, youth who are either themselves foreign-born and arrived as children or who are native-born with at least one foreign-born parent account for nearly one in five 15 to 34-year-olds, or 38.7 million people (OECD/EU, 2018[1]). Their share is increasing in virtually all OECD countries. How individuals, societies and policy makers refer to this crucial group is essential, though not always straightforward. The context of how and why a particular terminology is used is key to understand current practices and to initiate and frame policy change.

HOW?

Across OECD countries, strengthening the use of inclusive language in this context can take different forms:

- raise awareness of why terminology used to refer to youth with migrant parents matters, by supporting a discourse about adequate language given the national context
- avoid language and vocabulary that make full integration by definition impossible such as when talking about "migrant generations"
- promote the use of inclusive language by setting an example in policy documents and official statistics
- allow for self-identification of individuals and multiple identities in surveys

The first step to ensure inclusive language is to *raise awareness* about the role terminology plays for integration. Inclusive language can promote unity and make all people feel part of a group, hence integrated, by supporting individuals' self-perception as a vital part of their society (Collins and Clément, 2012[10]). Exclusive language is often used unintentionally. Labels, names and expressions can be created and used to portray certain groups as inferior or superior to others. Hence, becoming conscious of how language impacts other individuals and integration more broadly can help to prevent feelings of exclusion and discomfort. Policymakers can foster a trustful dialogue by avoiding word choices which may be interpreted as biased or demeaning and use inclusive language instead. Guidelines such as those developed by regional governments in Australia and Canada can support a respectful and inclusive discourse about appropriate terminology (Tasmanian Government, 2019[11]) (Government of British Columbia, 2018[12]).

Avoiding terminology that divides the resident population into "migrants" or "foreigners" on the one side and "natives" on the other is equally important. A prime example is talking about 'migrant generations', which makes full integration by definition impossible. This terminology, as used in many European OECD countries, also has several conceptional problems. For instance, "second-generation immigrants" perpetuates the migratory experience even for native-born children. The term usually refers to native-born youth with immigrant parents often with no distinction whether one or two parents migrated. In Spain, for example, the most common terminology used by governmental bodies is "immigrantes de segunda generación" while Italy uses the term "seconde generazioni di stranieri in Italia". According to the Italian Ministry of Labour, the expression refers to children of foreigners born or arrived in Italy in the first years of life. Similarly, in France the terms "jeunes issus de l'immigration" and "Seconde génération d'immigrés" refer to young descendants of immigrants. These terms apply to all youth with migrant parents with no distinction on their own place of birth. In the case of Germany, the term "Migrationshintergrund" (migration background) was introduced in official statistics in 2005. However, the concept is grounded in a mix of citizenship of the individual and country of birth. An Expert Commission to the Federal Government advised in early 2021 against the use of the term, because of both conceptual and statistical shortcomings (Fachkommission Integrationsfähigkeit, 2021[13]). Until 2016, the Netherlands similarly disregarded own migration experience, referring to individuals as "autochtoon", irrespective of their place of birth, if both parents were born in the Netherlands. The term "allochtoon" referred to individuals of whom at least one parent was born abroad. While these were deemed neutral terms when they were first introduced in 1971, they have become charged in everyday use and were dropped in 2016, following advice of the Netherlands Scientific Council for Government Policy (2017[14]). Going forward, the Council suggested to use 'residents with a migration background' and 'residents with a Dutch background' to distinguish when necessary. However, it also advised against reinforcing the social contrasts between established citizens and newcomers and adjust terminology based on context. In many countries, a debate remains regarding native-born offspring of immigrants, in particular those of mixed parentage. Austria, for example, uses the term "migration background", but counts children of mixed descent with an Austrian-born parent as "without a migration background". Similarly, in Denmark a person of 'Danish origin' is defined as a person who, regardless of their place of birth, has at least one parent who is born in Denmark and has Danish nationality.

Promoting the use of inclusive – or at least neutral – language starts with *setting a positive example in policy documents and official statistics*. "Native-born to foreign-born parents", the term used in most OECD documents on integration, refers to individuals born in the country and allows for a clear distinction of parental migration history. The term also acknowledges the fact that these persons are native-born and (in most cases) never migrated. Norway's official statistics, for instance, refers to "Norwegian-born to immigrant parents" to denote the native-born offspring of immigrants. In Canada, the population census indicates three terms to refer to the county's national population. "First-generation Canadians" are Canadians who were born outside Canada – so foreign-born. "Second-generation Canadians" are native-born children of immigrants who have at least one parent born outside Canada – reflecting the fact that their parents are generally Canadian citizens and thus integral part of the host-country society. Finally, "third-generation Canadians or more" refers to persons who were born in Canada to two native-born parents.

Allowing for self-identification of individuals is another way to allow language and terminology to depict a more adequate representation of an individual's identify then ascribed by others. In the Netherlands for instance, before the above described terminological changes, less than half of the native-born children of immigrants surveyed considered themselves as 'allochtoon'. There were also wide differences between different groups. Individuals seem to consider themselves less as allochtonen the more at home they felt in the Netherlands, the fewer the problems they had with the Dutch language, and the better their labour market position.

The United Nations Office of the High Commissioner for Human Rights (OHCHR) recommends that data disaggregated by ethnicity and migration should be based on self-identification, rather than through imputation or proxy (Office of the United Nations High Commissioner for Human Rights, 2018[15]). However, self-identification can change over time and may be partly context-specific, which hampers its use for monitoring over time.

2. Make sure all children start school on an equal footing

WHAT and WHY?

Ensuring that all youth can reach their full potential means levelling the playing field before children start school. OECD-wide, children of immigrants are overrepresented in socio-economically disadvantaged families. Early intervention is therefore crucial, as children who enter school with a relative disadvantage often struggle to catch up throughout schooling.

There is ample evidence that attending Early Childhood Education and Care (ECEC) benefits disadvantaged children, especially those with migrant parents (Balladares and Kankaraš, 2020[16]). It fuels children's social, linguistic and cognitive development and helps them overcome social disadvantage. Comparisons of the PISA reading scores of 15-year-old students with immigrant parents and similar socio-economic backgrounds show that those who attended ECEC consistently achieve higher scores. Overall, across the EU, the benefit of having attended preschool is 55 points at the age of 15 among the native-born children of immigrants – roughly equivalent to 1.5 school years. The corresponding benefit among native-born children of native-born is 23 points, about half a year of schooling (OECD/EU, 2018[1]). Most studies suggest that the critical age for ECEC participation to begin to show strong effects is around the age of three (OECD, 2017[3]).

In addition to mainstream ECEC, pre-school language screening and support can ensure that children of immigrants start school on equal footing with children of native-born. Many of the former speak a different or additional first language at home, contrasting most of their peers with native-born parents. Those who enter primary school without basic proficiency in the language of instruction, risk falling behind, since language mastery is a precondition for absorbing academic content and interacting with teachers and classmates. PISA data show that, at the age of 15, students with migrant parents who do not speak the language of instruction at home are approximately one year of schooling behind students with native-born parents (OECD, 2015[17]).

WHO?

Attending Early Childhood Education and Care (ECEC) is beneficial to all children. It yields particular benefits for children of immigrants from disadvantaged socio-economic backgrounds and who do not master the language well (Balladares and Kankaraš, 2020[16]). Despite ample evidence of these advantages, children of immigrants are still underrepresented in ECEC in many OECD countries (Figure 2.1). However, the ECEC participation gap to children with native-born parents has decreased over the last decade (OECD/EU, 2018[1]). Likewise, early language screening and support, ideally before school, is useful to identify potential training needs of all children. Children who do not speak the language of instruction at home or lack advanced vocabulary and literacy skills might require additional support beyond mainstream ECEC.

Figure 2.1. Early Childhood Education and Care (ECEC) attendance rates, by place of birth of parents or guardians

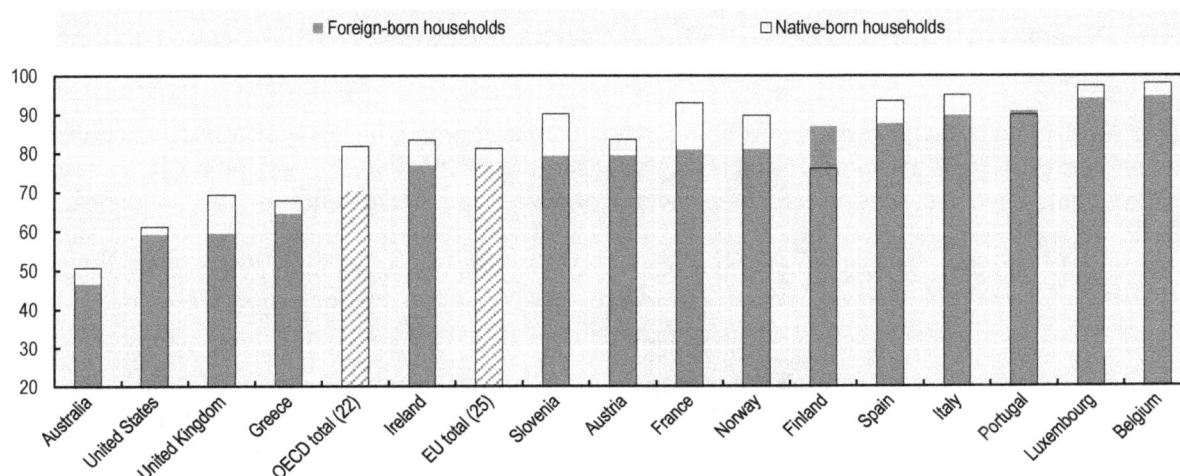

Source: OECD/EU (2018[1]).

HOW?

Policies to ensure all children start school on an equal footing can be broadly clustered into two approaches:

- increasing the participation of children of immigrants in Early Childhood Education and Care (ECEC)
- providing language screening and where necessary language support, at times including through the involvement of parents

The types of available ECEC services vary widely across the OECD. Important differences exist regarding the targeted age groups (0-3 years and 3-5 years), the management (public or private), the funding of services (free, subsidised or privately paid), the type of delivery (full-day versus part-day attendance) and the place of provision (in centres/schools or at home) (OECD, 2017[18]). To increase participation rates, three parameters are of interest:

- access: are ECEC services widely available and do immigrant children have access to them?
- affordability: is it possible to use ECEC services free of charge? If not, are there subsidies?
- awareness: are immigrant parents aware of the benefits associated with the use of ECEC and informed about available ECEC services in their area?

Most OECD countries expanded access to Early Childhood Education and Care since the early 2000s, and immigrant children have equally benefitted from this expansion (OECD, 2015[17]). In about two-thirds of OECD countries, children even have a legal entitlement to ECEC, at least from the age of three or four, generally regardless of their nationality or residence status. In the Nordic countries, Germany and Slovenia, children are legally entitled to a place in ECEC from the age of one or earlier. In Estonia and Latvia, children are entitled to a place starting at the age of 18 months, and Belgium guarantees access from 2.5 years of age. Another key parameter is the number of hours that children are legally entitled to. In about half of the countries the legal entitlement grants access to full-day services (40 hours per week or more), while in the other half, children are only entitled to childcare services for half a day (15-25 hours per week). A final parameter to ensure children of immigrant can access ECEC is local availability, so that transportation is not an obstacle (Neidell and Waldfogel, 2009[19]).

Box 2.1. Initiatives to include children from socio-economically disadvantaged families in ECEC programmes via home instruction

A prime and longstanding example of a home instruction programme for early childhood education is "Home Instruction for Parents of Pre-school Youngsters" (HIPPY). HIPPY, implemented in several OECD countries, teaches parents who face socio-economic disadvantage knowledge, confidence, and skills to nurture their children's readiness for school. Australia, for example, has implemented the programme in 100 disadvantaged communities. Across the country, more than 2 000 families benefit from a free, two-year home-based parenting and early childhood enrichment programme. Home tutors are available to help disadvantaged families implement the programme at home.

In the United States, the ParentChild+ programme provides low-income families with the skills and materials they need to prepare their children for school and life success. The programme offers twice-weekly visits to families with children between the ages of 16 months and four years. It employs early literacy specialists from local communities, who speak the language of the families with whom they work. They connect them to other community resources, such as health and medical facilities and other education programmes. Upon completion, the staff assist families in enrolling their child in a centre-based, pre-school programme. While the programme does not directly target immigrant families, 60% of the beneficiaries are families who have a home language other than English.

To ensure that ECEC are *affordable* and costs are not a barrier, the majority of OECD countries (about two-thirds) provide ECEC programmes free of charge. However, mirroring legal entitlement to ECEC, free programmes are often available only for children aged three years and older, while care options for those below three years of age tend to be funded, at least partly, by parental contributions (OECD, 2015[17]). Latvia (from 18 months) and Belgium (from 2.5 years) offer full access to free ECEC services below age three. However, for children from disadvantaged families – among which immigrant parents are overrepresented – access to ECEC is free of charge from birth in some regions of Austria, in the French Community of Belgium, in Chile, Finland and Luxembourg. Slovenia grants conditional free access to children from 11 months, while France entitles disadvantaged children aged two years and older to access free ECEC services. Countries that do not grant free access usually subsidise costs for ECEC. Some countries have programmes in place to reach children from socio-economically disadvantaged families at home (Box 2.1).

If parents are not *aware* of ECEC services or hesitant to use them, children of immigrants might not benefit from such services, even where widely available and affordable. Various OECD countries have developed initiatives to reach out to immigrant parents, and to raise parents' awareness of the value of early learning. Examples are home visit programmes, provision of learning resources and information to families, recruitment of culturally appropriate specialists, awareness campaigns, and trainings for pre-primary teachers and staff to work with culturally and linguistically diverse children (OECD, 2015[17]; OECD, 2014[20]).

Another way to ensure that children participate in ECEC is to make them compulsory. This is currently the case in 15 out of 36 OECD countries. Yet, in the vast majority of these countries, participation in ECEC is only compulsory from age five or later. For instance, Austria introduced a nation-wide free and compulsory half-day kindergarten year, one year before primary school. In France, Hungary, Israel and Mexico, ECEC is mandatory for all children from age three, and in Luxembourg compulsory ECEC starts at age four. In Switzerland ECEC up to the age 4 is not part of the compulsory education. However, at the age of four, all children attend a compulsory pre-school ("Kindergarten / pré-primaire ou école enfantine") for a duration of two years prior to primary school.

From a policy perspective, providing early support through high-quality ECEC is less costly and more effective than intervening at a later stage (Heckman, 2006[21]; Woessmann and Schuetz, 2006[22]). In countries where ECEC places are limited, increasing the available offer is thus likely to yield high pay-offs (Drange and Telle, 2015[23]). Where ECEC services are well established, informing immigrant parents and encouraging them to make use of these is a logical next step.

An equally vital prerequisite to ensure that all children enter school on an equal footing is language screening and support. This generally takes one of the following two forms:

- systematic language screenings and stimulation at pre-school age, usually provided through ECEC institutions and public health institutions
- systematic language screenings upon enrolment in primary school, complemented by follow-up assessments and support

Early language screenings before school are usually provided through ECEC or public health institutions. Frequently, these screenings are mainstream policy among all children, regardless of whether or not they have migrant parents.

Denmark, for example, routinely screens the language skills of all children at age three. Children with gaps receive compulsory language stimulation. Children in the United Kingdom undergo a routine language assessment at age two to three. A follow-up assessment is performed at the end of the 'Early Years Foundation Stage', which is usually the academic year in which children turn five. The objective is to support a smooth transition into 'Key Stage 1', which covers first and second primary school years when children are 5 to 7 years of age, and to help teachers plan an effective, responsive and appropriate curriculum meeting the needs of all children. Luxembourg assesses children's' language development at 30 months of age. If a screening reveals language difficulties, the country provides regular follow-ups and individual support until school age. In Norway, health clinics perform routine assessments of children's language abilities at age two and four, covering both children's first language and Norwegian. Clinics refer children with deficits to a follow-up assessment involving more extensive tests, diagnoses, and recommendations for tailored language support. In Germany, the age at which children are screened for language difficulties varies across states. The Land of Hesse, for example, performs routine language screenings in all ECEC institutions at the age of four. Where language difficulties are detected, children are referred to a follow-up screening at the public health department to consult with a paediatrician. Children with language difficulties receive one year of special support prior to entry into primary school in the form of a "preparation course" (Vorlaufkurs). Primary schools also assess language competency, usually upon entry. For children with deficits, ECEC institutions and primary schools jointly organise intensive, preparatory language courses in the year preceding primary school.

Austria carries out routine language screenings at the beginning and the end of each kindergarten year. ECEC staff observe children in every-day interactions at an ECEC centre and assess their language development against 15 criteria, including phonology, vocabulary, and ability to maintain a conversation. The results are used to develop tailored support offers, taking into account individual needs. In the Netherlands, young children from disadvantaged backgrounds aged two and a half to four years are entitled to participate in targeted early childhood education programmes (vooren vroegschoolse educaties) that provide ten hours of language development per week. For the remaining time, children attend regular early childhood education programmes. Findings from a national cohort study suggest that this approach bears high benefits in terms of better language mastery (Akgündüz and Heijnen, 2018[24]; Leseman et al., 2017[25]).

Once students reach the age of compulsory schooling, the responsibility for language development transfers from ECEC and health institutions to primary schools- Frequently, this is connected with a new language assessment. In Denmark, for example, immigrant children take part in an individual Danish language assessment upon enrolling in primary school to identify any need for additional support. For this purpose, the Ministry of Education developed a tool for teachers to assess the linguistic development of bilingual children in the language of instruction. Schools in New Zealand identify and assess the learning needs of students with difficulties in the English language. Specially trained resource teachers administer bilingual assessments through the 'Bilingual Assessment Service' (BAS). Schools receive funding for 'English as a second language' programmes for up to five years for students with migrant parents below a benchmark score (OECD, 2018[2]). National assessment standards of English Language Learning Progression (ELLP) allow to identify stages of learning and monitor immigrant students' progress from grade 1 to grade 13.

Table 2.1. Early language screening and stimulation

| | Early language screening before primary school | | | Early language stimulation for children in need before primary school | |
| | Yes/No | If yes age at … | | Yes/No | If yes, average number of hours per week |
		1st screening	2nd screening		
Australia	No	/	/	No (but pre-school language training in foreign languages through the 'Early Learning Languages Australia (ELLA) Programme')	/
Austria	Yes	3-6 years	1 year later	Yes	n.a.
Belgium	Yes	5 years	/	Yes (not systematic)	Varies
Canada	No	/	/	No (with the exception of British Colombia)	/ (3-8 hours in British Colombia)
Chile	No	/	/	No	/
Czech Republic	No (in individual cases only)	/	/	Yes	25 lessons per week
Denmark	Yes	2-3 years	Depends on municipality	Yes	30 hours per week
Estonia				Yes	
Finland					
France	No	/	/	No	/
Germany	Yes	Varies across regions (3-5 years)	/	Yes	Varies across regions and programmes
Greece	No	/	/	Yes	25 teaching hours per week (via kindergarten)
Hungary	Yes	5 years (or earlier according to local capacities)	5 years (if an earlier screening has been done before 5 years of age)	Yes	Minimum 2 lessons per week; maximum 45 minutes per lesson
Iceland					
Ireland	No	/	/	No	/
Israel					

	Early language screening before primary school			Early language stimulation for children in need before primary school	
	Yes/No	If yes age at ...		Yes/No	If yes, average number of hours per week
		1st screening	2nd screening		
Italy	No	/	/	No (not systematic but projects in selected kindergartens)	/
Japan					
Korea					
Latvia	No	/	/	No	/
Lithuania	No (but pre-school teachers evaluate children's development including communication skills at pre-school age)	/	/	No (but the general programme of pre-school teaching includes basic communication skills)	/
Luxembourg	Yes	2.5 years	Regulatory follow-ups are conducted until school age in case language difficulties are detected at first screening	Yes	8 hours per week
Mexico	Yes	Before 3 years	/	No	/
Netherlands				Yes	10
New Zealand	No	/	/	No	/
Norway	Yes	2 years	4 years	Yes	n.a.
Poland	No	/	/	No	/
Portugal					
Slovak Republic	Yes (for newly arrived children)	At age of arrival	Depends on individual needs	Yes	n.a.
Slovenia	No	/	/	Yes	n.a.
Spain					
Sweden	No	/	/	Yes	n.a.
Switzerland	No	/	/	Yes (not systematic)	Varies across cantons
Turkey	No	/	/	No	/
United Kingdom	Yes	2-3 years	5 years	Yes	n.a.
United States	No but children are screened when they enter the public school system, which could be (pre-)kindergarten or first grade)	/	/	No	/

Note: "n.a." = information not available; "/" = not applicable.
Source: OECD questionnaire on the integration of young people with migrant parents 2017.

Table 2.2. Early Childhood Education and Care

| | Starting age of compulsory education | Level of education | | Legal entitlement to a place in ECEC | | |
| | | Pre-primary | Primary | Yes/No | If yes … | |
					From age	Hours/week to which children are entitled
Australia	5-6 years		✓	Yes	4-5 years	15
Austria	5 years	✓		No	/	/
Belgium	5 years		✓	Yes	2.5 years	23.3 (Flemish community) 28 (French community)
Canada	5-6 years		✓	No	/	/
Chile	5 years	✓		Yes	4 years (under certain conditions from 0 years)	22
Czech Republic	5 years	✓		Yes	4 years	50
Denmark	6 years	✓		Yes	26 weeks	n.a.
Estonia	7 years		✓	Yes	18 months	n.a.
Finland	6 years	✓		Yes	0 years (from end of parental leave period)	50 (20 from 6 years onwards)
France	6 years		✓	Yes	3 years	24
Germany	6 years		✓	Yes	1 year	n.a.
Greece	5 years	✓		No	/	/
Hungary	3 years	✓		Yes	3 years	n.a. (all day service for 50 weeks/year)
Iceland	6 years		✓	No	/	/
Israel	3 years	✓		Yes	3 years	n.a.
Ireland	6 years		✓	Yes	3 years	15
Italy	6 years		✓	Yes	3 years	40
Japan	6 years		✓	No	/	/
Korea	6 years		✓	No	/	/
Latvia	5 years	✓		Yes	1.5 years	n.a.
Lithuania	6 years	✓		No	/	/
Luxembourg	4 years	✓		Yes	3 years	26
Mexico	3 years	✓		Yes	3 years	15-20
Netherlands	5 years	✓		No	/	/
New Zealand	6 years		✓	No	/	/
Norway	6 years		✓	Yes	1 year	41
Poland	6 years	✓		Yes	3 years	n.a.
Portugal	6 years		✓	Yes	3 years	40
Slovak Republic	6 years		✓	Yes	3 years	n.a.
Slovenia	6 years		✓	Yes	11 months	45
Spain	6 years		✓	Yes	3 years	n.a.
Sweden	7 years		✓	Yes	1 year	15-50
Switzerland	4 years in most cantons, 5 or 6 in others	✓		No	/	/
Turkey	6 years		✓	No	/	/
United Kingdom	5 years		✓	Yes	3 years	15
United States	Varies across states	Varies across states	Varies across states	No	/	/

Source: OECD (2017[18])European Commission/EACEA/Eurydice, (2016[26]) and OECD Secretariat analysis based on national legislation.

Table 2.3. Free access to Early Childhood Education and Care, 2016 or latest available year

	Legal entitlement to free access to ECEC			
	Yes/No	If yes …		
		From age	Unconditional free access	Conditional free access
Australia	No (but a means-tested subsidy is available)	/	/	/
Austria	Yes	0-4 years 5 years	✓	✓ (varies across states)
Belgium	Yes	0 years 2.5 years	✓	✓ (all registered jobseekers in training can be reimbursed for childcare)
Canada	No (but subsidised fixed fee service for everyone in Quebec and means-tested cash payments or tax credit in other provinces)	/	/	/
Chile	Yes	0 years 4 years	✓	✓
Czech Republic	Yes	5 years	✓	
Denmark	No (but subsidised and vouchers if family income is low)	/	/	/
Estonia	No (but subsidised)	/	/	/
Finland	Yes	0 years 6 years	✓	✓
France	Yes	2 years 3 years	✓	✓ (free in socially disadvantaged areas)
Germany	Differs across federal states	Differs across federal states	Differs across federal states	Differs across federal states
Greece	Yes	5 years	✓	
Hungary	Yes	3 years (in some municipalities from 4 months)	✓	
Iceland	No (but subsidised)	/	/	/
Israel	Yes	3 years)	✓	
Ireland	Yes	3 years	✓	
Italy	Yes	3 years	✓	
Japan	Yes	3 years		✓
Korea	Yes	3 years	✓	
Latvia	Yes	1.5 years	✓	
Lithuania	Yes	6 years	✓	
Luxembourg	Yes	0 years 3 years	✓	✓
Mexico	Yes	3 years	✓	
Netherlands	No (but parents can receive income-related tax allowances for childcare)	/	/	/
New Zealand	Yes	3 years	✓	
Norway	Yes	3 years		✓
Poland	Yes	5 years	✓	
Portugal	Yes	3 years	✓	
Slovak Republic	Yes	3 years	✓	

	Legal entitlement to free access to ECEC			
	Yes/No	If yes ...		
		From age	Unconditional free access	Conditional free access
Slovenia	Yes	11 months		✓
Spain	Yes	3 years	✓	
Sweden	Yes	3 years	✓	
Switzerland	Yes	4 years	✓	
Turkey	No (but subsidised)	/	/	/
United Kingdom	Yes	3 years	✓	
United States	Varies across states	Varies across states	Varies across states	Varies across states

Note: *Unconditional* free access refers to provision free of charge for all children of the concerned age group. Conditional free access means that free access is granted based on certain conditions, such as income, benefit entitlements, etc.

Source: OECD (2017[18])European Commission/EACEA/Eurydice, (2016[26]) and OECD Secretariat analysis based on national legislation.

3. Provide flexible education pathways for youth born abroad

WHAT and WHY?

Young people who arrive in the country past the start of primary education require flexible solutions. They face a higher risk of falling behind in the school system compared to their native-born peers and those who arrive at a younger age. In most countries, immigrant students who arrived at the age of 12 or older lag behind students in the same grade in reading proficiency at the age of 15 than immigrants who arrived at a younger age (OECD, 2015[17]). Evidence from Norway suggests that with every year a child spends outside the Norwegian school system before arrival subsequent educational and economic achievement decline (Bratsberg, Raaum and Røed, 2011[27]; Hermansen, 2017[28]).

Language is one key issue in this respect. A more demanding school curriculum requires a higher proficiency in the language of instruction. Those most in need of language support are students who migrate at compulsory school age and need to adapt to a new language of instruction immediately (Heath and Kilpi-Jakonen, 2012[29]). Research indicates that it takes children approximately two years to acquire communicative language skills. Still, it may take up to seven years for them to develop the academic language used in school environments (OECD, 2015[17]). Hence, the 'late arrival penalty' is higher when children migrate to a country where the language of instruction differs from their native language. What is more, in countries that sort students into different educational tracks and schools, recently arrived immigrants risk being sorted into an education track that mirrors their initial language level rather than their cognitive abilities.

Differences between educational standards in the origin and destination country are another challenge: the bigger the gap in the educational standards, the more late arrivals will have fallen behind (or moved ahead) compared to their peers in the destination country (Heath and Kilpi-Jakonen, 2012[29]).

A particular problem arises for youth who arrive towards the end of compulsory schooling age. These youth are at risk of failing to obtain a school leaving certificate in their new country in the limited time that remains. At the same time, they need to learn a new language and adjust to their new surroundings. Yet, for those who have educational credentials from their origin country, the transferral of credentials may also take time, putting these youth at a particular risk. Where late arrival results from restrictive family reunification policies, policy makers must balance the intended benefits of such policies against the costs in terms of lower educational outcomes for the children concerned (OECD, 2017[30]).

WHO?

Youth with migrant parents are a diverse group. The challenges they face as well as the support they may or may not require to succeed depend on many factors. One of them is their age at arrival. Those who arrive in the later years of lower secondary education from countries where the educational standards are lower and the language differs from that of the new country require particular attention. Without targeted and on-going support measures at school, they may not be able to obtain the basic skills needed to succeed.

HOW?

Countries should ensure that late arrivals have sufficient time to adapt to their new school environment and catch up with the demands of the new education system. The following approaches can mitigate the potentially negative effects of late arrival on educational attainment:

- adjusting mainstream education policy parameters, such as the school leaving age or the age at which students are sorted into different tracks
- establishing specific programmes for recently arrived students without proficiency in the language of instruction, such as time-bound reception or language classes
- providing recently arrived students and their parents with supplementary information and orientation on the schooling system and education environment, including in their mother tongue

Later *sorting into different educational tracks* can yield positive benefits for migrant youth, especially for late arrivals and in countries where ECEC is not well established. Separating students at an early age may lock late arrivals into a lower educational environment before they have had a chance to reach their full potential (Crul and Vermeulen, 2003[31]; Oakes, 2005[32]). In fact, early tracking brings disadvantages for students from lower socio-economic backgrounds more generally, who tend to be disproportionately assigned to lower tracks. This effect can be observed both in education systems that sort students into different schools and in school systems that sort students into different courses within the same school (Chmielewski, 2014[33]). Several OECD countries have raised or postponed the age of first tracking to the end of lower secondary education, to counter the negative impact of early selection. The Nordic countries were among the first to make that change in the 1970s, followed by Spain, some German states and Poland, where postponing the age of tracking in the early 2000s by one year to age 16 significantly raised the performance of students who would have been assigned to lower tracks, without worsening the results of top achievers (Wiśniewski and Zahorska, 2020[34]). However, in cases where it is neither realistic nor appropriate to change the system solely because of the difficulties of one group, higher permeability between tracks and adequate support are important remedies. Indeed, early sorting is less of an issue in education systems where students can change tracks relatively easily.

Along the same line of reasoning, some countries provide additional years of schooling beyond the usual school leaving age. Such solutions support immigrant students with limited formal education who arrive towards the end of compulsory education. In New Zealand, for example, late arrivals can remain in secondary education beyond the age of 19. The German state of Bavaria raised the compulsory age for vocational schools from 18 to 21, and in individual cases to 25, in reaction to the high inflows of refugee youth in 2015/16. Lithuania offers an additional year of schooling for late arrivals.

Many late arrivals, however, do not wish to pursue further education but prefer to take up employment, generally of the low-skilled kind. Targeted programmes combining studies with work experience can incentivise late arrivals to stay in education instead of looking for unstable, low-skilled jobs (Box 3.1). Finland's youth guarantee scheme provides an example of such a programme.

> **Box 3.1. Catch-up programmes for late arrivals outside mainstream education**
>
> In addition to targeted support offers in regular education institutions, some countries have developed specific catch-up programmes for recently arrived migrant students as an alternative to mainstream education.
>
> An example is the "Newcomer Schools Program" in the United States, which targets recent adolescent migrants with low levels of literacy, previous schooling, or English proficiency. Based on repeated English language assessments, the programme provides one to three years of first language development and second language instruction, lessons in core academic subjects, leisure time activities, development of skills for self-directed study, career counselling and an "email buddies" scheme linking newcomers with students from local mainstream schools. A further initiative in the United States is the non-profit 'Internationals Network for Public Schools'. The network designs, establishes and supports publicly funded secondary schools and programmes for newly arrived immigrant students who score in the bottom quartile on English language tests, in co-operation with public school districts. Network schools follow the same curriculum and receive the same amount of public per-student funding as other public schools. However, they provide extra resources and support to staff and students, mostly financed through separate fundraising. Students are taught in small groups and learning is structured in project-based activities, portfolios and internships, combining language and content instruction. The regular cut-off age is 21, but evening schooling options are available for working immigrant youth aged 15-24.
>
> Another example is the Young Migrant Education Program (YMEP) in Tasmania (Australia). YMEP provides recently arrived students aged 18-25 with English language training, teaches core subjects and develops general educational skills preparing newcomers for further study and employment. The programme, which also provides individual counselling and career support, is part of Australia's Technical and Further Education system, an alternative to mainstream education with a focus on vocational training.
>
> A further example of a specific programme for late arrivals is the "SchlaU-Schule" in Munich (Germany). The school enables young refugees – mainly unaccompanied minors – to secure secondary school leaving certificates through adapted teaching and individual support in a close-knit school setting. It also provides post-school follow-up into mainstream education.

Some countries initially place immigrant students in specific preparatory reception classes within regular education institutions before entering the mainstream classroom. These classes often focus on language learning and are used in about half of European OECD countries as well as in Japan. The idea is to teach late arrivals a minimum level of the language of instruction and to help them adapt to their new school environment before they transit to the mainstream classroom. Other countries immediately place recently arrived immigrant students into mainstream classrooms but ease their integration by providing additional language and content support beyond the regular curriculum. Poland, for example, provides up to five weekly hours of remedial instruction in Polish language and other core subjects to migrant youth with limited Polish language skills, for a maximum of 12 months following their arrival. Similar schemes exist in Hungary and Luxembourg. In Portugal, for instance, students with Portuguese language needs enrol in Portuguese as a second language classes and schools can benefit from additional teaching staff for this purpose. In cases with less than ten students with Portuguese language needs at a given school, students attend regular classes, but follow a specialised curriculum and benefit from support language classes. Besides, the Ministry of Education, in partnership with schools and the Portuguese Language Cyberschool, has developed distance courses in Portuguese as a second language (OECD, 2018[2]).

Postponing teaching of the curriculum until students master the language of instruction is controversial. Critics suggest that immigrant students fall even further behind their non-immigrant peers in such a settling and that language learning integrated in academic education is more efficient (Nusche, 2009[35]; Karsten, 2006[36]; OECD, 2010[5]). However, a certain adaption period is generally necessary for students who do not speak the language and/or face other obstacles. Fixed maximum durations of reception classes and tailored approaches ensure that immigrant students do not get stuck. Reception classes can, for example, start as a full-time support programme and phase out as students gradually integrate into mainstream education. In Sweden, for instance, migrant youth undergo an assessment of their level of academic knowledge within two months of arrival. Based on this assessment, the school decides on the student's grade and placement in either introductory (separate) or regular classes. Further, the school designs an individual education plan covering Swedish language and core academic subjects. The transition to mainstream education follows on a subject-by-subject basis. Foreign-trained mother-tongue tutors or language teachers are more and more common as teachers in reception classes, including recently arrived migrants themselves. This approach, a part of Sweden's 'fast-track' integration pathways for certain professions, enables migrant teachers to obtain employment while their foreign teaching qualifications are being assessed for official recognition. A similar programme exists in Norway.

Outside of reception or language classes, several countries provide targeted support offers of a more generic orientation type. In Canada, schools run school readiness programmes, such as a 'Newcomer Orientation Week' (NOW) for immigrant and refugee high school students and 'Welcome & Information for Newcomers' (WIN) for elementary and junior high school students. The programmes introduce newcomer students to facilities, routines and policies, and provide contacts and support before the academic year starts. Teachers, settlement workers and peer leaders provide mentorship to build relationships, reach academic goals, enhance social and language skills, and connect with the broader community. A similar programme exists in Australia, where newly arrived immigrant students can take part in a peer-led youth orientation called 'Settle Smart'. The programme connects newcomers with peer educators of the same age, who inform about education pathways and social life in Australia.

In addition to language of instruction and orientation support, some OECD countries also enable students with migrant parents to learn their parents' native languages at school. Austria, for example, provides systematic training in some origin languages. Instruction of the language of the origin country of the parents is offered as an optional subject voluntarily at primary and secondary schools and taught between two and six hours per week. In the school year 2015/16, 32 900 students participated in such instruction. The vast majority were in primary school, where more than a quarter of all students with another mother tongue than German attended instruction in the language of parental origin. In Belgium, key origin countries support the extra-curricular language training. The programme 'Opening to Languages and Cultures' (OLC) enables children to study Chinese, Spanish, Greek, Italian, Arabic, Turkish, Portuguese and Romanian two hours per week in addition to the regular curriculum. Courses are open to all students in primary and secondary schooling irrespective of their nationality and cover language and culture of the origin country. Parental origin countries recruit and pay for teachers. This, however, results in limited possibilities for oversight of the host-country educational institutions.

Table 3.1. Specific reception classes for recently arrived youth in OECD countries, 2016

	Yes/No	Targeted educational level / age group	Duration	Criteria for transition to mainstream classes
Australia	No	/	/	/
Austria	No (except in some regions)	/	/	/

	Yes/No	Targeted educational level / age group	Duration	Criteria for transition to mainstream classes
Belgium	Yes	Primary and secondary education (2.5 – 18 years)	1 week – 18 months	If the teacher considers the student ready for transition, an integration council decides whether to integrate her/him in a class according to her/his level
Canada	Not at the national level but most provinces provide targeted support to students (incl. newcomers) with enhanced language or academic needs)	n.a.	n.a.	n.a.
Chile	No	/	/	/
Czech Republic	No (but plan to establish 'strategic classes' for disadvantaged students at primary schools)	/	/	/
Denmark	Depends on municipality			
Estonia				
Finland	Yes	Primary and secondary level	Max. one academic year (900 hours for 6-10 year-olds, 1 000 hours for students above 10 years of age)	Student's progression in subjects taught
France	Yes	Primary and secondary education (6 – 16 years)	12 months	Reaching a certain language level
Germany	Yes	Primary and secondary education	6-12 months	Reaching a certain language level
Greece	Yes	Primary Education	1-3 academic years depending on the education priority zone of school	Following the regular curriculum without language problems
Hungary	No	/	/	/
Iceland				
Ireland	No	/	/	/
Israel				
Italy	Not systematically	/	/	/
Japan	Yes	Primary and secondary education (7-15 years)	Depends on the child's Japanese language ability	Reaching a certain language level
Korea				
Latvia	No	/	/	/
Lithuania	Yes	Primary and secondary education	Up to one academic year	Reaching a certain language level
Luxembourg	Yes	Mainly secondary (12-16 years) but also primary education	One academic year	Reaching a certain language level
Mexico	No	/	/	/

	Yes/No	Targeted educational level / age group	Duration	Criteria for transition to mainstream classes
Netherlands	Yes	Primary level	One academic year	Reaching a certain language level
New Zealand	No	/	/	/
Norway	Yes	6-18 years	n.a.	Reaching a certain language level
Poland	No	/	/	/
Portugal				
Slovak Republic	No	/	/	/
Slovenia	No	/	/	/
Spain	No (but existed until 2011)	(Primary and secondary level)	/	/
Sweden	Yes	Primary and secondary level	Up to two years	Student's progression in subjects taught (transition is subject-based)
Switzerland	Yes (but varies across regions and demand)	Varies across cantons	Usually up to one year	Varies across cantons
Turkey	No (but pre-school, primary, secondary and higher education options for Syrian refugee students in temporary protection centres)	/	/	/
United Kingdom	Varies from school to school	n.a.	n.a.	n.a.
United States	Yes	Primary and secondary level	Until English language proficiency is reached (not limited)	English Language Proficiency (ELP) assessment, additional criteria may be used, but do not substitute for a proficient score on an ELP assessment

Note: n.a. = information not available; / = not applicable. In many OECD countries such as Germany and the United States, education is predominantly a subnational competence. The measures mentioned here might only apply to some states/entities.
Source: OECD questionnaire on the integration of young people with migrant parents 2016.

Table 3.2. Targeted support offers for late arrivals in OECD countries, 2016

	Targeted support offers for late arrivals	
	Yes/No	Type of support
Australia	No (not at national level, depends on state/ territory governments)	States/territories may fund activities such as: • Intensive English language classes in the first months • Intensive English language schools preceding enrolment in local schools • Bridging support between intensive English language support and mainstream secondary school
Austria	Yes	• Additional German language training and free dictionaries • Learning support including free tutoring, homework support and free private lessons
Belgium	No	/
Canada	Yes	School readiness programs including mentorship, such as the Newcomer Orientation Week (NOW) for newly arrived high school students and Welcome & Information for Newcomers (WIN) for elementary and junior high school students
Chile	No	/
Czech Republic	No	/
Denmark	Depends on municipality	
Estonia		
Finland	Yes	Extra 100 hours of preparatory training in reception classes
France	No	/
Germany	Yes	• Specific reception classes or special transition classes within vocational schools that aim at

	Targeted support offers for late arrivals	
	Yes/No	Type of support
		reaching a minimum school leaving diploma • Recognition of native language to substitute a 2nd or 3rd foreign language • Additional years of schooling if necessary
Greece	Yes	• Reception classes in secondary education • Reception structures for the education of refugees living in refugee accommodation centres • Extra tuition classes in primary education and lower secondary education for students who have attended reception classes but still have problems in attending regular classes
Hungary	Yes	• Additional language training and catch-up lessons in main subjects for one year • Possibility to repeat a grade
Iceland		
Ireland	Yes	Language support for students in need
Israel		
Italy	Yes (not systematic)	Training in Italian as a second language
Japan	Yes	Free of charge enrolment in junior high school for those who have not completed compulsory education
Korea		
Latvia	Yes	• Systematic and obligatory assessment of the language skills, the subjects taken, and the learning achievements of new arrivals at enrolment into primary or secondary education (assessment may include parents, childcare institutions and experts) • Elaboration of a tailored learning programme and support measures for a period of one to three years with a view to enable newcomer students to obtain compulsory education (grade 9)
Lithuania	Yes	Additional year of schooling
Luxembourg	Yes	One to two years of additional support in language, maths and social integration (plans to extend the period of support to three or four years)
Mexico	No	/
Netherlands		
New Zealand	Yes (but not systematic)	• Possibility to remain in secondary school beyond the age of 19 as an adult student as a bridge or preparation for further studies • 1-2 years of additional literacy and numeracy training • English language support for up to 5 years • In-class and one-on-one support from bilingual tutors and liaison officers
Norway	No	/
Poland	Yes	Remedial classes in Polish language and other subjects for up to 12 months
Portugal		
Slovak Republic	Yes	Assistance helping late arrivals to achieve lower secondary education
Slovenia	Yes	Possibility to postpone admission to the first grade for one year and adjustment of teaching and assessment methods for up to two years
Spain	No	/
Sweden	Yes	Introductory education as preparation for upper secondary school or equivalent adult education
Switzerland	Yes (but not systematic)	Varies across cantons
Turkey	No	/
United Kingdom	Varies from school to school	n.a.
United States	Yes	Specific schooling options for newcomer students (e.g. Newcomer Schools Programme or Internationals Network for Public Schools)

Note: "n.a." = information not available; "/" = not applicable. In many OECD countries such as Germany and the United States, education is predominantly a subnational competence. The measures mentioned here might only apply to some states/entities.
Source: OECD questionnaire on the integration of young people with migrant parents, 2016.

Table 3.3. Training of origin country languages at school in OECD countries, 2017 or latest available year

	Training in origin country language at school		
	Yes/No	Education level or age group aimed at	Part of or additional to regular curriculum
Australia	Yes (for certain languages including Arabic, Chinese, French, German, Hindi, Indonesian, Italian, Japanese, Korean, Modern Greek, Spanish, Vietnamese, Turkish)	Up to grade/year 10	Part of regular curriculum
Austria	Yes	Compulsory schools and academic secondary schools (lower and upper level)	Optional subject, additional to regular curriculum
Belgium	Yes (for Chinese, Romanian, Spanish, Greek, Turkish, Italian, Portuguese, Arabic, but not systematic)	All levels	Additional to regular curriculum
Canada	Not systematically (but exceptions in certain provinces, such as Vancouver)	/	/
Chile	No	/	/
Czech Republic	No	/	/
Denmark			
Estonia			
Finland	Yes (52 languages, not systematic)	Basic and general upper secondary level	Optional subject in addition to regular curriculum (not systematically provided)
France	Yes, international teaching of foreign languages (EILE) and teaching of language and culture of origin (ELCO)	/	/
Germany	Yes	Primary and secondary level	Optional subject, part of regular curriculum
Greece	No (not on a systematic basis)	/	/
Hungary	No (except at schools for national minorities, foreign schools and bilingual schools)	/	/
Iceland			
Ireland	Yes (for certain EU languages, Russian, Arabic and Japanese)	Secondary level	Optional (non-curricular) subject in leaving certificate examinations
Israel			
Italy	No (not systematic)	/	/
Japan			
Korea			
Latvia	No	/	/
Lithuania	Yes (for national minority languages such as Russian, Polish and Belorussian)	Primary, lower and upper secondary level	Part of regular curriculum
Luxembourg	No	/	/
Mexico	No	/	/
Netherlands	Yes (Turkish and Arabic)	Secondary level	Optional subject additional to regular curriculum
New Zealand	No (but some schools run afternoon sessions in students' native languages if community provides funding)	/	/
Norway	Yes	Age 6-18	Part of regular curriculum
Poland	Yes (not systematically, organised and financed by foreign diplomatic establishments or cultural organisations)	Age 6-16	Additional to regular curriculum
Portugal			

	Training in origin country language at school		
	Yes/No	Education level or age group aimed at	Part of or additional to regular curriculum
Slovenia	Yes	Basic and upper secondary schools (and pre-schools for Italian and Hungarian minorities)	In addition to regular curriculum
Slovak Republic	No	/	/
Spain	No	/	/
Sweden	Yes	Primary and secondary schooling	Instruction in origin country language is an extracurricular offer but can in certain cases replace a second foreign language
Switzerland	Yes (on a voluntary basis and not systematic)	Grade 1-9 / primary and lower secondary level (may vary across cantons)	Additional to regular curriculum
Turkey	Yes	n.a.	n.a.
United Kingdom	No	/	/
United States	No (but high school equivalency exams can be taken in Spanish)	/	/

Note: "n.a." = information not available; "/" = not applicable. In many OECD countries such as Germany and the United States, education is predominantly a subnational competence. The measures mentioned here might only apply to some states/entities.
Source: OECD questionnaire on the integration of young people with migrant parents, 2017.

4. Involve immigrant parents in the education process

WHAT and WHY?

Parental support is critical to children's education outcomes. Students are more likely to remain in school and perform successfully if their families are well informed and involved in their education (Wilder, 2013[37]; Borgonovi and Montt, 2012[38]). However, immigrant parents tend to be less likely to be connected with their child's school community (OECD, 2018[2]). Various barriers can prevent immigrant parents from maintaining regular contact with their school and teachers. For instance, they might have low levels of education themselves, face language barriers or lack knowledge about the functioning of the education system (Antony-Newman, 2018[39]). As a result, they may be unable to intervene at the right time and to adequately support their child's learning at home.

WHO?

Immigrant parents frequently have higher aspirations for their children's educational outcomes than native-born parents (Hagelskamp, Suárez-Orozco and Hughes, 2010[40]; Becker and Gresch, 2016[41]). In a study of four European countries, immigrants also assigned a higher value to education than non-immigrants (Hadjar and Scharf, 2018[42]). Further, parents' psychological engagement and behavioural involvement appears to have a stronger effect than parental socio-economic and education levels on immigrant children's achievement-related motivation and achievement (Kim, Mok and Seidel, 2020[43]). Nevertheless, high aspirations are not sufficient when actual knowledge on how to overcome disadvantage and attain educational goals is lacking. Indeed, many immigrant parents, especially in Europe, have low levels of formal qualification and/or lack knowledge about the host-country education system. As a result, the intergenerational transmission of disadvantage is often higher for immigrants than for comparable native-born (OECD, 2017[3]).

HOW?

Efforts to involve immigrant parents to support their children's education can take various forms. The most common types are

- reaching out to immigrant parents in a proactive manner to provide information on the education and school system, the child's performance in school as well as possibilities for parental involvement
- strengthening immigrant parents' skills to enable them to support their children's learning

The most obvious way to *reach immigrant parents* is via the school itself. Schools can, for example, provide translations of documents about the education system, about the development of the child's behaviour and performance in school and about opportunities for parents to get involved in school activities. They can also arrange regular meetings between teachers and parents and provide childcare for the duration of the session. An example is the French initiative 'Parent`s Tool Box' (La mallette des parents), which provides schools with educational guidelines and a structured set of topics. This approach allows teachers to discuss with parents during regular meetings to build trust and encourage parents to engage in their children`s education. Meetings happen around pivotal moments in the school trajectory, such as the transition from primary to lower secondary education. The scheme was piloted in 2008 in urban areas with a high concentration of migrant students and has since been rolled out widely across French public schools.

Schools can also reach parents with the support of dedicated liaison staff who maintain a working relationship with them. In Canada, elementary and secondary schools with large newcomer populations may include settlement workers from community agencies, funded under the federal government's Settlement Workers In Schools (SWIS) initiative. SWIS workers reach out to immigrant parents, help them understand the school system, support their children's education and deal with challenges that may arise. Along similar lines, the New South Wales Department of Education in Australia provides Community Information Officers to help schools strengthen links with immigrant parents and communities. (OECD, 2015[17]).

Another way to inform immigrant parents is via municipal authorities. In New Zealand, for example, recently arrived refugee parents have a meeting with a senior education advisor in their local community. This advisor introduces them to New Zealand's school system and explains how they can support their children's education.

In some cases, the easiest way to reach immigrant parents is via another migrant parent who speaks their language. Based on this idea, various mentoring programmes have been developed across the OECD that train immigrant parents to visit and advise other immigrant parents in education matters. An example are the ´neighbourhood mother' or ´district mother` programmes that exists in Denmark, in the Netherlands, in various parts of Germany and Austria (OECD, 2017[30]). In Norway, the Multicultural Initiative and Resource Network follows a similar approach. The volunteer organisation raises awareness about the importance of parental support in education among immigrant parents. It encourages bilingual parents to co-operate with schools to facilitate the learning of bilingual students more general (OECD, 2018[2]).

Efforts to *strengthen immigrant parents` skills* aim at helping migrant parents engage their children in learning activities linked to their school curriculum. Typically, these programmes focus on host-country language acquisition and literacy training and are often small-scale programmes at the local level. In Boston (United States), the Intergenerational Literacy Project (ILP) provides English literacy support to immigrant parents. With this support, they can support their children's literacy development and also have a forum through which adults can share their family literacy experiences. The programme is based on a partnership between Boston University and surrounding urban communities. It seeks to improve immigrant students' chances of to attain the objectives of their schools and to reinforce positive attitudes towards education more generally. In the German city of Hanover, elementary schools organise biweekly meeting groups ('backpack parent groups`) for immigrant parents. During these sessions at their children's school, parents learn about the topics taught in their child's class. The groups also teach them host-country language skills and encourage them to participate in school activities. The meetings are tutored by immigrant parents with host-country language proficiency, who have completed a 9-months training module. Sessions take place during school hours and include childcare for younger children. Similar programmes exist in several Austrian states and Luxembourg ("Sac d'histoire"). France has a large-scale national initiative to "open the school for parents for the success of the children" (Ouvrir l'école aux parents pour la réussite des enfants) which provides language training in schools for parents to help them better understand the education system. The training is provided in 2x2 hours per week, for a total of 60 to 120 hours per year, in groups of 12-15 participants. The programme is jointly financed by the Ministry of the Interior and the Ministry of Education. Detailed information on the programme is available in nine languages. Video films explaining the French education system are also available in these languages.

Projects that strengthen migrant mothers will also convey benefits for their children, albeit the link is more indirect – across generations. In Germany, the initiative "Strong in the work place – Migrant mothers get on board" campaigns for better opportunities for migrant mothers. Over 90 nationwide contact points offer coaching, qualification or language practice, as well as contacts to find gainful employment. Since 2015, the initiative has reached over 14 000 mothers and about two thirds of former participants are in employment, in the process of gaining additional skills or qualification recognition after completing the programme (German Federal Ministry for Family, Seniors, Women and Youth, 2021[44]).

An alternative way to foster migrant parents' language and literacy skills is to provide courses in which parents and children participate together. Programmes of this type exist in several countries, including in Austria, Denmark, Ireland, Italy, Slovenia and Sweden. Vienna, for example, runs a learning support programme for immigrant mothers, who can learn German in parallel with their children at their ECEC centre or school. Other projects involve immigrant parents in further learning activities. New Zealand, for example, provides refugee families and secondary school-aged children with computer literacy training, a computer and a one-year internet connection through the "Computer in Homes" programme.

Table 4.1. Initiatives to involve immigrant parents in their children's education in OECD countries, 2016

	Yes/No	Type of instrument
Australia	No (with few exceptions)	Resources may be developed by a range of organisations, with and without government funding (e.g. after an initial government funded pilot project "*Connecting CLD Parents*" the non-for-profit Centre for Multicultural Youth developed and funded a resource kit "*Opening the School Gate. Engaging culturally and linguistically diverse parents in schools*" and later created state-specific editions in conjunction with State Governments)
Austria	Yes	•Home Instruction for Parents of Preschool Youngsters (HIPPY) • Parental education facilities •DVD and brochure in various origin country languages informing about possibilities for parental involvement in school (e.g. parent representatives) • Language training programmes for mothers at schools
Belgium	Yes	
Canada	Yes	Settlement Workers in Schools (SWIS) help families (immigrant parents and guardians) understand the school system and support their children, as well as receive referrals to other community resources
Chile	No	/
Czech Republic	n.a.	n.a.
Denmark	Yes (not systematic)	E.g. Outreach activities to involve parents via the "We Need All Youngsters" campaign
Estonia		
Finland		
France	No (except small-scale pilots)	/
Germany	Yes	• Co-operation between schools, administration and migrant organisations • Information material in different languages • Information and advice about VET options in the framework of the KAUSA initiative • Support to migrant associations and projects that work with and engage with migrant parents • Special integration courses for parents combining language training with instruction about the school system and connecting parents with teachers
Greece	Yes	Monthly meetings with parents in primary schools and training programmes on parents' literacy, children's health education, parents' involvement in pupil's homework, etc.
Hungary	No	/
Iceland		
Ireland	Yes	• Family involvement training programmes • Host country language training for parents at their children's school

	Yes/No	Type of instrument
		• Training in using public libraries
Israel	Yes	Family involvement training programmes
Italy	Yes (not systematic)	• Information sessions • Reach out activities • Encounters with parents • Joint mother-child training groups for Italian as a second language ("classroom moms" or "mothers to school")
Japan		
Korea		
Latvia	No	/
Lithuania	No	/
Luxembourg	Yes	• Provision of information through systematic radio broadcasts in Portuguese and English language • Project *sac d'histoires* providing literacy support to and involving parents in schools for children aged 6 to 8 years
Mexico	No	/
Netherlands	Yes	Family involvement training programmes
New Zealand	Yes (but not systematic)	• Bilingual liaison workers assist schools in making contact with families and communities (funded through *Refugee Flexible Funding Pool*) • Refugee parents meet with senior education advisors in local community
Norway	Yes	Grant scheme for municipal parental guidance services used by health stations, schools and child welfare services including: • Group discussions • Information sessions • Home assignments
Poland	Yes	Annual competition for public projects to counteract intercultural conflicts at schools through developing co-operation between the school community and the parents of students with migrant parents, especially of refugees
Portugal		
Slovak Republic	Yes	Cooperation between schools and parents
Slovenia	Yes	• Translated information material to parents of kindergarten children about the education system and the rights and duties of children and parents • Encouragement of parents to participate in the school/kindergarten's work and activities and to learn Slovenian language together with their children
Spain	Yes	
Sweden	Yes (but not systematic, depends on municipality)	• Reach out activities, information sessions • Family involvement training programmes • Host country language training for parents together with their children • Training in reading children's books and use of public libraries
Switzerland	Yes (part of cantonal integration programmes)	Varies across cantons
Turkey	No (but in development)	Various modules are planned at Public Educational Centres including: • Parenting Education Course Program • Father Support Training Program • Child Nutrition • Child activities for 0-3 years • Family Support for 0-36 month children who are under developmental risk
United Kingdom	Yes	Individual schools may run initiatives (e.g. "Key to Integration" programme providing language training to mothers and involving them in school communities)
United States	Yes	Funding to schools for family literacy programmes, parent outreach, and training activities for migrant parents

Note: n.a. = information not available.
Source: OECD questionnaire on the integration of young people with migrant parents 2016.

5. Reduce the concentration of disadvantaged youth with immigrant parents

WHAT and WHY?

Youth with migrant parents are often concentrated in certain neighbourhoods and schools. Evidence on the impact of concentration of youth with migrant parents in schools is not clear-cut. The literature for the United States and Europe suggests that this concentration hinders the school performance of other youth with migrant parents. However, such concentration seems to have little to no impact on youth with native-born parents (Schneeweis, 2015[45]). A key variable in this context is not the migrant status in itself, but the large share of youth who come from socio-economically disadvantaged households and the resulting concentration of disadvantage in schools.

The concentration of disadvantaged youth with immigrant parents in schools is a particular challenge in European OECD countries, where significant shares of the immigrant population lack basic qualifications. For instance, in France, Germany, Greece and Belgium, students with migrant parents in schools with a high concentration of students with migrant parents perform around 40 points lower in mean PISA scores than their peers in low-concentration schools – the equivalent of one year of schooling (OECD, 2017[3]); in some countries the gap is even significantly larger. However, this gap largely disappears when the socio-economic background of their parents is taken into consideration. An example is Denmark, where the performance of youth almost evens out once these characteristics are controlled for (Beuchert, Christensen and Jensen, 2020[46]). In practice, however, it is difficult to disentangle the two, as migrant families often account for a disproportionate share of the most disfavoured. By contrast, in Australia and Canada, where immigrants are overrepresented among the highly educated, children – whether with immigrant or native-born parents – perform better when they find themselves in a school with many children of immigrants.

WHO?

OECD-wide, almost three in four 15-year-old students with migrant parents go to schools where at least a quarter of their classmates also have migrant parents, and more than one in five where over three-quarters do. Such concentration can be detrimental if – and only if – coupled with low education background of the parents (OECD/EU, 2018[1]).

Figure 5.1. How different factors affect academic performance

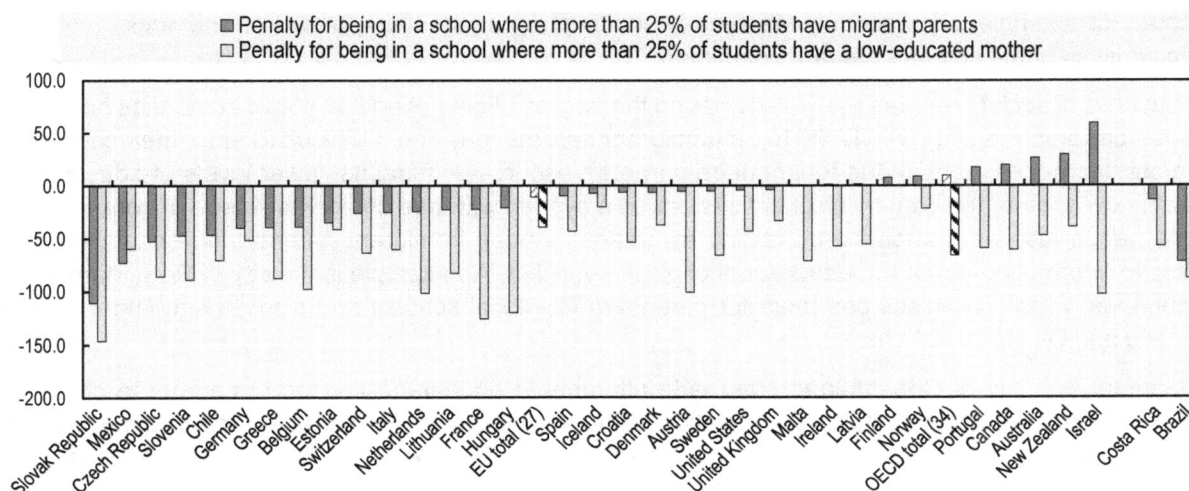

Note: Difference in PISA mean scores for 15-year-old pupils in schools above the 25% threshold and those in schools below the 25% threshold, 2015.
Source: OECD/EU (2018[1]).

HOW?

Policy efforts to address the problems associated with a concentration of children of immigrants from disadvantaged socio-economic backgrounds in the same schools can broadly cluster into two approaches:

- preventing the concentration of disadvantaged youth with migrant parents in the same schools
- mitigating the negative consequences of such concentration, including through additional funding and teaching support

Policy attempts to *prevent concentration* can take various forms. Some countries have established mechanisms to allocate students equitably across different schools. For example, countries can design school areas in such a way that they include a heterogeneous mix of more and less affluent neighbourhoods. Another approach is to transfer students between schools if the concentration of specific socio-economic characteristics becomes too high. Policies can also influence (enhance or limit) the possibility for parental school choices.

In the municipality of Aarhus, Denmark's second-largest city, all bilingual pupils about to enrol in school are required to take a Danish language test. If they test below a predetermined threshold they lose their free school choice and the municipality assigns them to a school. If the school lies outside the student`s school district, local authorities provide free bus services between home and school. A recent evaluation of this policy finds that this forced form of busing has a negative effect on the academic performance and well-being of bilingual pupils (Damm et al., 2020[47]). Italy also aims to achieve a balanced distribution of foreign-born students across schools and classes through agreements between schools, the formation of school networks and co-operation with local authorities. Schools and classes where more than 30% of students do not speak Italian are identified as targets of intervention. However, meeting or exceeding this target level does not result in an automatic intervention.

Limits to the extent to which popular, oversubscribed schools can select students based on performance or socio-economic status is another way to ensure an equitable distribution of students across schools.

One way to do so is to make school choice plans subject to simple lotteries (Godwin et al., 2006[48]). Another way is to provide financial incentives for oversubscribed schools to accept students with migrant parents. For example, several countries allocate funding, amongst others, based on the socio-economic characteristics of the school's student population.

The success of such measures partly depends on the degree of discretion that public authorities have over parental decision-making (OECD, 2010[5]). Immigrant parents may find it difficult to enrol their children in the most appropriate school due to language barriers, resource constraints, lower levels of education or lack of knowledge of the country's school system. In a system with free choice, the issue of concentration should hence also be addressed by raising awareness among immigrant parents and enhancing their access to information about the educational choices available. An example is the city of Rotterdam in the Netherlands, which organises bus tours for parents to visit local schools and discuss enrolment options (Brunello and De Paola, 2017[49]).

In Denmark, the city of Copenhagen has made attempts to encourage immigrant parents to choose a school with a predominant student population without children of immigrants. Participating schools provided specific preparation and training for teachers and provide for an integration specialist or a translator with a migration experience. The same approach has also been tried vice-versa, namely encouraging non-immigrant parents to send their children to schools with many students who have migrant parents. Copenhagen, for example, not only targeted migrant parents but simultaneously initiated publicity campaigns and collaborations with kindergartens in order to convince native-born Danes to enrol their children in local schools with a significant immigrant population. A similar example is the project 'School in zicht' in the Flemish part of Belgium, which motivates native-born parents to enrol their children in local schools with a high concentration of migrant students.

Mitigating negative impacts of concentration of disadvantaged students on students' learning is an important focus. OECD countries have taken different steps to improve the learning environment and the quality of education in schools where the concentration of disadvantage is already above the national average. Such steps may include allocating additional funding or supplementary teaching staff, attracting qualified teachers to schools in need, and qualifying teachers to better respond to the needs of students with migrant parents.

Many countries provide additional government funding and resources to schools with a high share of students from low-educated or immigrant families. Depending on the country, such financing may be only available for specific purposes such as language training or reception classes or freely attributable according to each school's needs.

In Switzerland, schools in the Canton of Zurich receive professional support and funding of around EUR 34 000 per year if more than 40% of their students are foreign nationals (excluding Germans and Austrians) or speak another language at home than one of the official Swiss languages. The funds are allocated in the framework of an obligatory area-wide model of quality assurance entitled 'Quality in multicultural schools-QUIMS'. The scheme aims to raise the quality of schools with large shares of students with migrant parents (OECD, 2018[2]). An evaluation suggested that the scheme improved the writing proficiency of students across all grade levels and positive outcomes in reading ability and transition to secondary education and vocational training. However, QUIMS schools still underperform compared with other schools in both respects (Roos, 2017[50]; Canton of Zurich, 2017[51]).

New Zealand allocates funding to schools for additional initiatives to meet the needs of students whose parents are refugees. Such financial support includes bilingual tutors in mainstream class programmes as well as education co-ordinators and liaison workers to assist schools in making contact with families and communities, and supporting refugee homework centres. Funding can also target specific projects rather than schools. In Austria, the nation-wide "Lerncafe" project offers free tutoring, homework support and afternoon care programme for 6 to 14-year-old children from a disadvantaged background, of which the vast majority have migrant parents. In 2016/2017, 95% of the participating children completed the school year successfully. Evidence on the previously described busing policy in Aarhus, Denmark, suggests that school resources can more than compensate for potential negative peer effects in schools with high concentration of youth with migrant parents (Damm et al., 2020[47]). Teachers are the most important resource of schools and ensuring high-quality education in disadvantaged schools requires the best teachers. Teaching staff can make a difference in the learning and life outcomes of otherwise similar students. Yet, disadvantaged schools often struggle to attract and retain the best prepared and experienced teachers (OECD, 2018[52]; Hanushek, Rivkin and Schiman, 2016[53]). Several OECD countries introduced incentives such as higher salaries or more attractive working conditions, to attract and keep qualified teachers at schools serving disadvantaged students. The evidence on the effectiveness of such schemes is mixed. Evaluations of a bonus scheme in France in the early 2000s found that boni had no effect on turnover rates and attracted mostly inexperienced teachers (Bénabou, Kramarz and Prost, 2009[54]). In contrast, evidence from the United States suggests that higher salaries increased teacher mobility. However, the research also finds that teacher mobility is much more strongly related to student achievement and ethnic background (Hanushek, Kain and Rivkin, 2001[55]). Yet, if salary increases are substantial, they can make a larger difference. In North Carolina (United States), a USD 1 800 retention bonus for certified teachers who work in disadvantaged schools reduced teacher turnover by 17%. Retention of teachers results in savings of roughly USD 36 000 per teacher who did not move schools (OECD, 2012[56]). Korea, too, attracts teachers into disadvantaged schools through additional salary. Besides, smaller class size, less instructional time, extra credit towards future promotion and the ability to choose the next school where one works play a role. Evidence suggests that disadvantaged students in Korea are more likely than advantaged students to be taught by high-quality mathematics teachers (Schleicher, 2014[57]).

Financial and other incentives are only effective if teachers are competent to work with immigrant students from disadvantaged backgrounds. Results from the OECD's Teaching and Learning International Survey (TALIS) indicate a need for professional development in this area (OECD, 2015[17]). While teacher training usually addresses topics associated with teaching in a multicultural setting, there is rarely a coherent and systematic curriculum for this. A country that has made efforts to change this is the United Kingdom. In 2004, the Department for Children, Schools and Families introduced a professional development programme to increase primary teachers' confidence and expertise to meet the needs of bilingual students. The scheme produced promising results in language skills but did not affect math and sciences competencies (Benton and White, 2007[58]). Norway, too, has encouraged competence development regarding multicultural issues in the education sector.

Beyond financial and training support for the regular teaching staff, some countries also provide additional support staff in schools with many youth of immigrant parentage. In Canada, the federally funded Settlement Program provides an array of settlement and integration supports for newcomers to Canada, including targeted supports for youth and their families. The Settlement Workers in Schools (SWIS) initiative places settlement workers in schools with large newcomer populations to act as liaisons between newcomer students, their families, the school system, and the broader community. SWIS workers provide a variety of supports, including outreach to newly arrived families; information and orientation; and needs assessments and referrals. In addition, Settlement Program services can include social connection, recreational, and employment supports targeted to newcomer youth.

Table 5.1. Additional funding for schools with disadvantaged students in OECD countries, 2016

	Yes/No	Budgeted costs	Targeted education or age level	Eligibility criteria for receiving additional funding
Australia	Yes	n.a.	n.a.	Funds are allocated through the 'English Language Proficiency loading programme', which targets students with limited English language proficiency (students must come from a language background other than English

	Yes/No	Budgeted costs	Targeted education or age level	Eligibility criteria for receiving additional funding
				and have at least one parent who completed school education only to year 9 or below)
Austria	No (but additional teaching staff for schools with high share of non-German speaking students)	/	/	/
Belgium	Yes	EUR 8 002 412	Kindergarten, primary and secondary educations	• Per capita income • Level of education • Unemployment and activity rates • Recipients of the minimum guaranteed monthly income • Professional activities • Housing standards
Canada	No	/	/	/
Chile	No	/	/	/
Czech Republic	Yes	n.a.	Primary school	Request for subsidies filed by school
Denmark				
Estonia				
Finland	Yes (so-called "positive discrimination funding")	n.a.	n.a.	n.a.
France	No	/	/	/
Germany	Yes (but earmarked for personal of reception classes and support offers for students in mainstream classes)	n.a.	Primary and secondary education and vocational schools	Students' need for specific support, presence of recently arrived students
Greece				
Hungary	Yes (provided by the Institution Maintenance Centre (KLIK) from its own centralised budget)	n.a.	n.a.	Needs based (e.g. for employing teachers for Hungarian as a foreign language)
Iceland				
Israel				
Ireland	Yes	EUR 110.27 million (2016)	Pre-school to second-level education (3 to 18 years)	Level of disadvantage in school
Italy	Yes	• EUR 1 million (2015/16; Ministry of Education) • EUR 13 million (2014-20; AMIF)	Primary and secondary education	• Implementation of specific projects eligible for funding • Share of foreign-born youth in school (for funds from Asylum, Migration and Integration Fund, AMIF)
Japan	Yes	JPY 140 000 000	Kindergarten to secondary education	Request from local government
Latvia	Yes (Social and Pedagogical	EUR 927 656 (Jan – Aug 2016)	Grade 1 -12	Schools with children from disadvantageous families and juvenile offenders (funding depends on number of

	Yes/No	Budgeted costs	Targeted education or age level	Eligibility criteria for receiving additional funding
	Adjustment Programmes)			students in adjustment programs; coefficient 1.1 is applied to calculate public funding for adjustment programs)
Lithuania	Yes	EUR 1 742 per student	Primary or secondary education (for immigrants or returnees during first year at school)	Earmarked for integration classes (if there are at least 5 migrant students) and support measures in mainstream classes
Luxembourg	Yes	• EUR 45 665 980 • EUR 188 588 (for schools enrolling asylum seekers)	Primary and secondary education	High share of socially disadvantaged learners in community/school (high correlation with migrant population)
Mexico	No	/	/	/
Netherlands	Yes		Primary education	Socio-demographic characteristics of the student population measured via parental education level
New Zealand	Yes	NZD 859 000 +GST (additional refugee specific initiatives)	Secondary education (9 – 13 years)	Students with refugee background status
Norway	No	/	/	/
Poland	No	/	/	/
Portugal	Yes	n.a.	n.a.	Disadvantaged context, high rate of school failure and dropout
Slovak Republic	Yes	n.a.	n.a.	Students requiring additional language training
Slovenia	Yes (for add. teachers, learning materials, field-trips, bilingual instruction, Slovenian language training)	n.a.	Basic schooling (ISCED 1 and 2)	• Number of Roma students • Number of bilingual classes • Number of SEN students and the scope of determined support
Spain	No (but existed until 2011)	(n.a.)	(Primary and secondary education)	(Foreign-born profiles of the education institution)
Sweden	Yes	n.a.	Pre-, primary and upper secondary school	Compensation to municipalities for immigrant students is built into the municipal equalisation system to ensure equal financial footing
Switzerland	Yes (not systematic)	Varies across cantons	Varies across cantons	Varies across cantons
Turkey	No	/	/	/
United Kingdom	Yes	GBP 2.5bn in 2016 (GBP 1 320 per primary age and GBP 935 per sec. age student)	Primary and secondary education	• Pupil premium for disadvantaged students (mainly pupils from low income households) • Separate discretionary local funding for students classed as having *English as an Additional Language*, who have been in the school system for a maximum of 3 years)
United States	Yes	USD 737 400 000 (incl. funds ear-marked for reception classes, add. teaching staff in main-stream classroom and targeted offers for late arrivals)	Primary and secondary education	Number of immigrant and English language learner students in each State

Note: n.a. = information not available; / = not applicable. In many OECD countries such as Germany and the United States, education is predominantly a subnational competence. The measures mentioned here might only apply to some states/entities.

Source: OECD questionnaire on the integration of young people with migrant parents 2016.

Table 5.2. Allocation of additional teaching staff in the mainstream classroom and incentives for teachers to work in schools with disadvantaged students in OECD countries, 2016

| | Additional teaching staff in mainstream classroom | | Incentives for teachers | |
	Yes/No	Criteria for allocation	Yes/No	Type of incentives
Australia	No	/	Yes ("Teach for Australia" programme placing high quality candidates, known as Associates, in disadvantaged secondary schools)	• Reduced teaching load • Support and training • Award of accredited postgraduate teaching qualification
Austria	Yes	Total number of recently arrived students with insufficient German language proficiency in a federal state	No	/
Belgium	Yes	• Secondary schools: selected disadvantaged schools benefitting from special resources (*encadrement différencié*) • Primary schools: criteria not specified	n.a.	n.a.
Canada	Yes	Number of English/French language learners and students requiring enhanced language support	No	/
Chile	No	/	No	/
Czech Republic	No (but assistants (not prof. teaching staff) can be added at primary schools; plan to introduce prof. teacher co-workers)	/	Yes	Additional salary
Denmark				
Estonia				
Finland	Possible (but not systematic)	n.a.	n.a.	n.a.
France	No	/	Yes	• Additional salary • Smaller class size and better student to teacher ratio • Less instructional time • Facilitation of future promotion
Germany	Yes (in many federal states)	• Minimum share of foreign-born in classroom • Minimum share of students in need of language training, regardless of background	No	/
Greece				
Hungary	No	/	Yes	Bonus pay schemes
Iceland				
Israel				
Ireland	Yes	Enrolments	No	/
Italy	No	/	No (but teachers involved in specific projects for migrant	/

	Additional teaching staff in mainstream classroom		Incentives for teachers	
	Yes/No	Criteria for allocation	Yes/No	Type of incentives
			students receive an hourly reimbursement)	
Japan	Yes	Decision of local board of education	No	/
Korea	n.a.	n.a.	Yes	• Additional salary • Smaller class size • Less instructional time • Additional credit for future promotion • Choice of next school
Latvia	No	/	No (but specific training is provided for teachers working in multicultural contexts)	/
Lithuania	Not systematic	/	n.a.	n.a.
Luxembourg	Yes	Newly arrived students with insufficient proficiency of instruction language (Luxembourgish at preschool level, German / French at primary level)	Yes	Reduced number of students per class (15 instead of 25)
Mexico	No	/	No	/
Netherlands				
New Zealand	No (but funding for bilingual tutors to support mainstream class programmes)	/	No	/
Norway	No (but mainstream policy)	Mainstream policy targeting primary and lower secondary schools with >20 students per teacher and scores below national average (not migrant specific)	No	/
Poland	Yes	No specific criteria (students in need of support are entitled to a teacher assistant in their native language for 12 months)	Yes	• Bonus for difficult working conditions • Smaller class size • Additional teacher with qualifications in special education
Portugal				
Slovak Republic	Yes (assistant teachers)	Students with language barriers	Yes	Personal awarding
Slovenia	No	/	Yes	Smaller group size in schools (or lower child/adult ratio in ECEC)
Spain	No (but existed until 2011)	(Foreign-born profiles of the education institution)	Yes	• Smaller class sizes • Recognition of extra-work ("merits") to facilitate transits to other schools
Sweden	Yes	• Student's needs • Decision of the head teacher	Yes	State grants for additional salaries for skilled teachers in certain urban areas with a high level of exclusion
Switzerland	Yes (not systematic)	Varies across cantons	No	/
Turkey	No	/	Yes	• Smaller class sizes • Bonus payment for teaching language courses to foreign students

	Additional teaching staff in mainstream classroom		Incentives for teachers	
	Yes/No	Criteria for allocation	Yes/No	Type of incentives
United Kingdom	Yes (not systematic)	School's decision based on specific student needs	Yes (not systematic)	• Teach First programme • Payments, financial assistance, support or benefits
United States	Yes	n.a.	No (not systematic across the country)	/

Note: n.a. = information not available; / = not applicable. In many OECD countries such as Germany and the United States, education is predominantly a subnational competence. The measures mentioned here might only apply to some states/entities.

Source: OECD questionnaire on the integration of young people with migrant parents 2016.

6. Prevent school drop-out and establish second-chance programmes

WHAT and WHY?

The first step for successful labour market integration is to ensure everyone leaves school with the necessary skills to succeed, including a qualifying diploma. However, migrants who arrived as young children are over-represented among the 15-24 year-olds who leave school prematurely in most OECD countries. School drop-outs lack minimum credentials for both successful labour market entry and for further education and training opportunities. Not surprisingly, therefore, they face a high risk of becoming inactive or unemployed and are prone to long-term social and economic disadvantage. In all OECD countries – with the exceptions of the settlement countries, Israel, Italy, Latvia and the United Kingdom – children of immigrants are more likely to be not in employment, education or training (NEET) than their peers with native-born parents (OECD/EU, 2018[1]).

Where prevention and early intervention fail to avoid early school leaving, second-chance programmes allow youth to obtain a basic qualification and find a way into the labour market. Such programmes offer alternative pathways. These can lead back into mainstream education, or prepare early school leavers to integrate into vocational education and training (VET) to obtain a professional qualification.

WHO?

OECD- and EU-wide, drop-out levels of immigrant offspring are similar to those of young people of native-born parentage at 7% and 9% respectively. In contrast, 11% of foreign-born youth who arrived as children in the OECD leave school early, and the share of drop-outs is 15% in the EU. Moreover, the native-born children of immigrants are more likely than their peers with no migrant parents to drop out in the majority of European countries, while the reverse is the case in the settlement countries (OECD/EU, 2018[1]).

Second chance programmes generally target early school-leavers who lack basic qualifications or those with a basic certificate who struggle to enter VET or find a job. Such measures rarely target youth with migrant parents specifically, but cater youth in need more generally. However, youth with migrant parents are often overrepresented among the target group.

Figure 6.1. Early school leavers

Percentages, 15- to 24-year-olds, around 2016

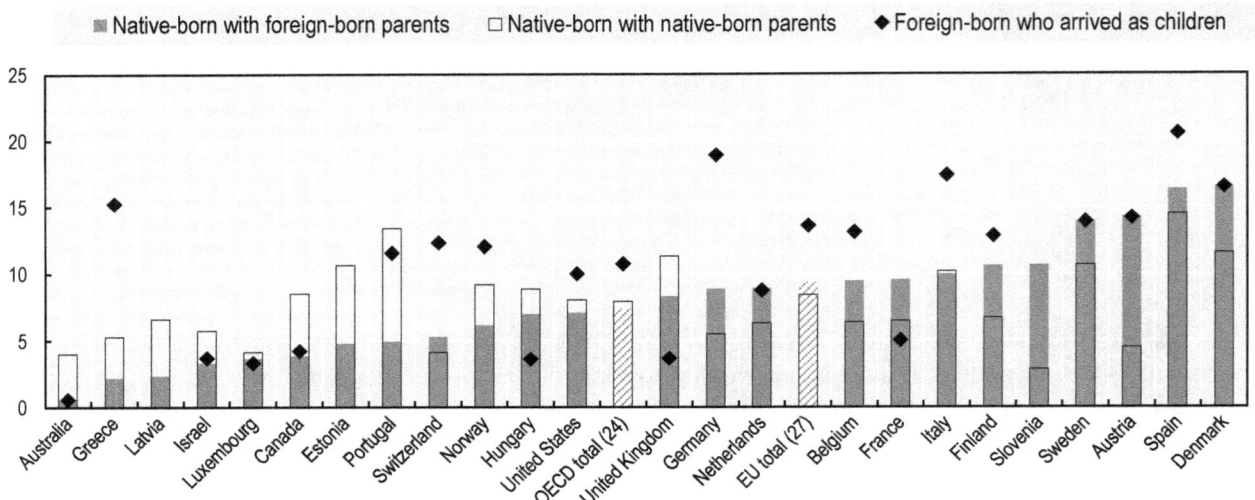

Source: OECD/EU (2018[1]).

HOW?

Policy efforts to ensuring that youth with migrant parents leave the education system with a qualifying diploma broadly cluster into two approaches:

- preventing early school dropout and tackling early school leaving at the systematic and individual level
- establishing comprehensive second chance programmes including alternative educational routes to higher education and improving high-quality apprenticeship opportunities

Preventing early school dropout and tackling early school leaving involves addressing its causes at the systemic level of the education system as well as targeting specific high-risk groups at the individual level. Measures at the *systematic level* typically include expanding and promoting the use of high-quality early childhood education and care, postponing educational tracking, limiting the use of grade repetition and raising the minimum official school leaving age for compulsory education (Lyche, 2010[59]; De Witte et al., 2013[60]; Nouwen, Clycq and Uličná, 2015[61]; European Commission, 2013[62]).

In Europe, the European Union encourages member countries to address common risk factors for early school leaving. The goal is to lower the average dropout rate to less than 10% by 2020 at different levels of the education circle. Typically, these measures focus on students from disadvantaged backgrounds, including – but only rarely specifically targeting – youth with migrant parents.

Among the few countries to have set up schemes that specifically target students with migrant parents is Denmark. Since 2003, the country has been running the "We Need All Youngsters" campaign to support 13-20 year-old youth to complete their education. The initiative initially focused on youth with migrant parents exclusively, but has been expanded to help struggling youth regardless of their background by enhancing their professional, social and personal skills through homework assistance; role model groups;

internships; and fairs informing about available VET opportunities. The campaign also promotes parent involvement in educational choices. Since 2011, 'We need all Youngsters' has focused on boys.

Another example of a dedicated programme to tackle school drop-out among youth with migrant parents is the Austrian programme 'Integration Ambassadors`. As part of the broader "Together Austria" initiative, the scheme encourages successful young migrants to become ambassadors of integration and pay visits to schools and associations to motivate other youth with migrant parents to see education as an opportunity and to make use of existing career options.

In Portugal, the 'Choices Programme' (Programa Escolhas) promotes the integration of 6 to 24 years old from disadvantaged social backgrounds, many of whom are immigrant descendants. The programme involves local authorities and civil society organisations. It includes several strategic areas of intervention, including combatting early school drop-out through the creation of new educational tools; the development of personal, social and cognitive skills through formal and non-formal education; and the promotion of family co-responsibility in the parental surveillance process. The current seventh round (2019-20) aims to benefit about 50 000 youth.

Measures to retain youth in schools at the individual level involve targeted interventions to support at-risk students and institutions. Approaches typically include case-by-case mentoring, tutoring and initiatives to engage parents in their children's education. Such a personalised approach is expensive and not easy to deliver, but the costs that would arise if these youth fail to complete education and do not integrate into the labour market are much higher.

Where preventive intervention comes too late, second-chance programmes provide school drop-outs and other youth with an opportunity to catch up. Some programmes enable participants to obtain an occupational qualification. Others focus on preparing youth to reintegrate into mainstream education and training programmes. Successful second-chance programmes display several characteristics that distinguish them from mainstream education. These include a focus on individualised teaching methods; flexible and needs-based curricula; holistic assessment approaches; small classes with low student-teacher ratios; multi-professional teams supporting learners, welcoming learning environments; and partnerships with mainstream education institutions, local communities and employers (UNICEF, 2017[63]). Youth with migrant parents often benefit more from mainstreamed support tools for all underachieving students than from targeted migration -history-specific approaches, found a review of second-chance programmes in the EU (European Commission, 2014[64]). However, these have to be adapted, notably with respect language training where needed.

In Slovenia, the PUM-O programme helps young people ready themselves for re-entering formal education or finding a job. Length of participation is adjustable to individual needs. The programme operates with small groups of 15-20 youth with an average age of 19-20 supported by three mentors. While not specifically targeted to them, shares of youth with migrant parents are growing (OECD, 2017[65]). In Germany, the Joblinge programme trains, mentors and connects young people with the labour market. Participants who have on average been out of school for two years before joining the programme, are mostly between 16 and 25 years of age and over two-thirds have migrant parents. Based on a close collaboration with regional employers, individual mentorship and skills training the programme supports youth to find their own vocational training place or job. Since 2016, the programme runs a specific stream for refugees, which offers additional language classes and job trial periods for young refugees (Joblinge Foundation, 2018[66]). In Flanders, second-chance education (Tweedekansonderwijs) is part of the formal adult education system and is provided by the Centres for Adult Education. It offers early school leavers the opportunity to obtain a degree of secondary education based on a modular structure and evening courses. It also allows young adult learners to set out their individual learning path. As a financial incentive, graduates are paid back their tuition fees when obtaining a diploma (OECD, 2019[67]). While available to all youth, by the nature of the programme youth with migrant parents are a key group among those eligible.

Many school dropouts prefer low-paying, unstable and often informal work over schooling; especially for those with parents from countries where labour market entry at a young age is common. Second-chance programmes can combine studies with work experience and labour market measures to address the incentives faced by youth with migrant parents to privilege work over education. Sweden, for example, has introduced an education contract in 2015 to encourage unemployed youth between the ages of 20 and 24 to return to adult education to gain an upper-secondary qualification. The agreement increases the financial aid available while offering increased flexibility to combine studies with work and labour market initiatives. The initiative does not explicitly target youth with migrant parents. Still, they are likely to be among the primary beneficiaries given their overrepresentation among those who do not qualify for upper-secondary education (OECD, 2016[68]).

Table 6.1. VET bridging programmes and second chance offers for school drop-outs, including young people with migrant parents in OECD countries, 2016

	Yes/No	Type of programme
Australia	Yes	• *Transition to Work* service (administered by Department of Employment) provides intensive pre-employment assistance to young people who have disengaged from work and study and are at risk of long-term welfare dependence. The service is designed to improve the work readiness of young people aged 15 to 21 years of age and help them get into work (including apprenticeships and traineeships) or education. • Pilot programmes in Sydney, Brisbane and Melbourne (administered by the Department of Social Services) support young refugees and other vulnerable migrants under 25 years of age to stay engaged in education and make successful transitions to employment through i) addressing barriers to employment; ii) accessing vocational opportunities; iii) staying engaged with education; iv) building social connections through sport.
Austria	Yes	• *Initiative adult education:* Joint federal-provincial programmeenabling youth to acquire basic literacy and numeracy skills or to take a compulsory school leaving exam (not exclusively for youth with migrant parents); approx. EUR 7.5 million funds in 2014 • *Production schools* preparing for regular VET or apprenticeships through training workshops in crafting, social and career counselling, internships and basic skills training; approx. EUR 26 million funds in 2015
Belgium	Yes	• *Services d'Accrochage Scolairse (SAS):* 3-6 months temporary social and academic reintegration support for school dropouts • *Work-Up* project: (Migrant) youth counsellors support Flemish Public Employment Service in reaching out to unemployed migrant youth
Canada	Yes	*Canada Youth Employment Strategy:* Funding for employers who provide skills and knowledge development ('Skills Link'), career guidance and work experience ('Career Focus') and summer job opportunities ('Canada Summer Job') to youth facing barriers to employment
Chile	No	/
Czech Republic	No	/
Denmark	Yes	Preparatory basic education and training (FGU)
Estonia		
Finland	Yes	Foreign-language vocational upper secondary education and training combining Finnish or Swedish as a second language and vocational training
France	Yes	• Promotion of VET programmes • Second Chance Schools providing vocational training, individual coaching and traineeships to unemployed early school leavers
Germany	Yes	• Introductory training (development of basic employability skills through e.g. long-term (6-12 months) company placements with subsidised pay and social insurance contributions) • Early starter programme: Employment agency supports 25-35 year-old adults to obtain a professional qualification and basic skills and pays them a premium after successful completion of the interim and final exams; 120 000 prospective participants between 2016-20 • Vocational orientation, guidance and placement into training • Career entry support through mentoring • Training-related assistance and assisted vocational training • Vocational preparation schemes (attainment of apprenticeship entry maturity)

	Yes/No	Type of programme
Greece	Yes	• Second Chance Schools targeting young adults (not exclusively immigrants) who have not completed compulsory education (budget of 3.6 million for Jan-Jul 2016) • Life-long Learning Centres (Kentra Dia Viou Mathisis) operated by municipalities in the framework of Continuing VET (CVET) that offer training programmes (including language training) to all persons in need (not exclusively targeted at immigrants) (budget 23.7 million for Apr 2012 – Sep 2016) • The "Odysseas" education programme in Greek language, history and culture for immigrants (budget EUR 9.7 million Oct 2008 – Nov 2015) • The "Triptolemous" education programme promoting employment of young (primarily unemployed) people in the agricultural sector
Hungary	Yes	Vocational Training Bridge Programmes assist students in joining secondary education or vocational training or prepare them for employment (EUR 48 680 total budgeted expenditures for 2016-20)
Iceland		
Israel		
Ireland	No	/
Italy	Yes	Main competences and funding on education system are at regional level. Promotion for VET programmes are equally open to nationals and non-nationals. Second chance schools provide vocational training, individual coaching and traineeships to unemployed early school leavers. 2014-20 EU Youth Guarantee scheme supports an increasing number of young people not in education or employment.
Japan	No	/
Korea		
Latvia	Yes	3-9 months vocational education programs within the Youth Guarantee Programme for young people aged 15-29 years
Lithuania	No	/
Luxembourg	Yes	• Training focused on competence-based and modular qualifications incl. guidance and access to labour market (over 6 000 courses provided, including evening classes) • VET programmes in English language
Mexico	No	/
Netherlands	Yes	*Step to Work Programme*: One-year work placement with a private sector employer along with preparatory courses and ongoing training (joint venture of municipalities, PES and social partners)
New Zealand	Yes (not systematic)	n.a.
Norway	Yes	*Programme for increased completion (of Upper Secondary Education and Training)* involving research projects and administration of regional networks to share best practice, funded jointly by federal government and counties
Poland	No	/
Portugal	Yes	• Specific employability support structures (GIP) for unemployed immigrant youth and young adults helping them define and develop their path of integration or reintegration into the labour market through: Professional information and support in active job search Disclosure and referral to job offers and training Placement activities Information and referral to support measures for entrepreneurship, employment and training Information about community programs to promote mobility in employment and vocational training in Europe Motivation and support for participation in temporary occupations or activities on a voluntary basis Periodic presentation control of the beneficiaries of employment benefits Personalised follow-up of the unemployed people during the integration or reintegration phase • *Chances Programme*: reintegrated into school, employment or vocational training
Slovak Republic	No	/
Slovenia	No	/
Spain	Yes	*PCPI -Initial Vocational Qualification Programme*: •Combination of basic general and vocational education for students who failed or are at risk

	Yes/No	Type of programme
		of failing the compulsory secondary schooling exam •Possibility to obtain a compulsory school leaving diploma
Sweden	Yes	• Introductory programmes (including VET) for teenagers inupper secondary education • VET courses in municipal adult education (part of the ordinary education system) • Trainee Jobs – allows youth with incomplete education to combine work (subsidised) and study for a vocational certificate • Education contract – to encourage unemployed youth between 20-24 to return to adult education to gain an upper secondary qualification. The contract increases financial aid while increasing flexibility to combine studies with work and labour market initiatives
Switzerland	Yes	Varies depending on the partner organising the programme (e.g. Motivation Semester)
Turkey	No (but scholarships for foreign students to attend regular VET programmes)	/
United Kingdom	Yes	n.a.
United States	Yes (not specific for youth with migrant parents)	*US Job Corps Programme*

Note: n.a. = information not available.
Source: OECD questionnaire on the integration of young people with migrant parents 2016.

7. Promote educational excellence and role modelling

WHAT and WHY?

Youth with migrant parents need to be able to excel in the educational system. They are often very motivated and have high aspirations for their education and career – higher than youth with native-born parents (OECD, 2018[2]). They are 8 percentage points more likely than students with native-born parents of similar socio-economic status and academic performance to aspire to complete tertiary education, and 11 percentage points more likely to expect to pursue a high-status career, such as working in managerial and professional occupations (OECD, 2015[17]).

Yet, native-born children with low-educated immigrant parents in many European countries are less likely to complete upper secondary school, compared with their native-born peers at similar levels of parental education (OECD, 2017[3]). Regarding tertiary education, the picture is more diverse. In many countries, including in OECD Europe, youth with migrant parents are more likely to attend university than their peers with native-born parents who have a comparable socio-economic status (Aydemir, Chen and Corak, 2013[69]; Kristen, Reimer and Kogan, 2008[70]; Richardson, Mittelmeier and Rienties, 2020[71]). On the other hand, there are strong differences between groups of youth with parents from different countries, with some experiencing barriers to pursue higher education (Camilleri et al., 2013[72]). There is also a notable underrepresentation of youth with migrant parents in access to the most prestigious universities (Shiner and Noden, 2014[73]; Boliver, 2013[74]).

A key element to support young people's development are role models. However, for effective role modelling, individuals must perceive role models to be similar to themselves. This similarity regards not only their aspired education and career path but also their social background and migration history (Valero, Keller and Hirschi, 2019[75]; Karunanayake and Nauta, 2004[76]; Zirkel, 2002[77]; Buunk, Peiró and Griffioen, 2007[78]). A longitudinal study with 12 to 14-year-old students in the United States, for example, found that having at least one ethnic- and gender-matched role model was associated with improved academic performance (Covarrubias and Fryberg, 2015[79]).

WHO?

Role models are particularly relevant for native-born youth of immigrant parents in situations where negative stereotyping or discrimination prevail.

Figure 7.1. Highly educated by parents' place of birth

Percentages, 25- to 34-year-olds not in education, around 2017

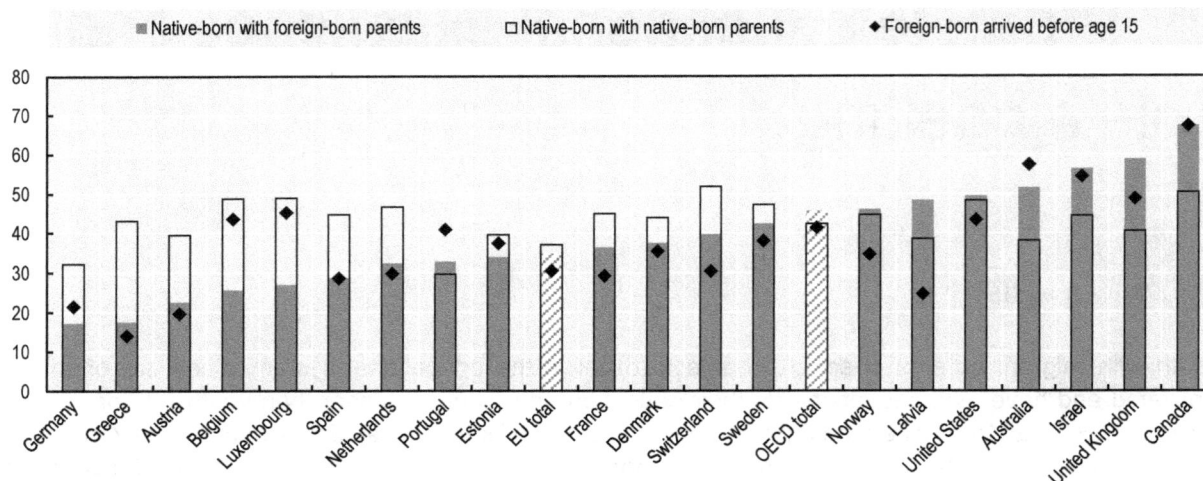

Source: OECD/EU (2018[1]).

HOW?

Increasing the representation in prestigious education pathways and in the public domain can occur in several ways:

- Encouraging higher education institutions to attract youth with migrant parents into their programmes
- Providing students with migrant parents with role models, for example via peer-mentoring schemes
- Using the public sector as a role model by pro-actively promoting recruitment of candidates with migrant parents and encouraging immigrants and their children to apply to public-sector jobs

Various OECD countries *encourage universities and other higher education institutions to attract youth with migrant parents* into their programmes. An example is Australia, where the state Government has implemented targeted measures to increase the acceptance and participation of children of immigrants in higher education. The Victorian Tertiary Admissions Centre, for example, runs a Special Entry Access Scheme that grants students from a non-English speaking or refugee background. In Finland, the government implemented targeted measures to design student-selection processes that account for the specific circumstances of youth with migrant parents, made efforts to develop open higher education institutions and provides funds for student guidance for this group. Besides, higher education institutions can apply for state support in the form of study vouchers to assist students in improving their Finnish language proficiency (OECD, 2018[2]). In many other countries, including Germany and France, certain prestigious higher education institutions and scholarship programmes have specific initiatives to attract youth with migrant parents.

Mentoring programmes are an effective way to provide children of immigrants with role models. In such schemes, students in higher education or young professionals with migrant parents coach and support younger students. These schemes often feature regular training for mentors, structured joint activities for mentors and mentees and a focus on parent involvement as well as formulated programme objectives. Where they have been implemented, such programmes often proved highly effective (OECD, 2010[80]).

An example is the 'Young Role Models' (*Junge Vorbilder*) peer mentoring scheme, which operates in the German city of Hamburg. The programme brings together lower secondary school students with migrant parents and university students of the same parental language for tutoring, socioemotional support as well as educational and vocational orientation. Mentoring can take the form of group sessions in secondary schools, or it can be conducted individually at the mentees` home. Mentors receive ongoing training and benefit from information about education-related topics, including scholarship and internship opportunities. Similarly, the Nightingale Mentoring scheme in Sweden pairs up university students with 8 to 12-year-old children from countries where participation in higher education is very low. Mentors and mentees build a personal relationship meeting every week for one school year. The goal is to improve social skills, school performance and ultimately raise the child`s likelihood of applying for university. Started in 1997, the scheme has since been implemented in Austria, Finland, Germany, Iceland, Norway, Spain and Switzerland.

The public sector, in particular, can play an essential role in promoting the integration of immigrants and their children by employing young adults with migrant parents. Public sector employment of youth with migrant parents generates several benefits. First, the presence of civil servants with migrant parents enhances diversity within public institutions, making them more representative of the communities they serve. Second, how the wider public perceives immigrants and their children depends in part on their 'visibility' in public life and the contexts in which they become 'visible'. Teachers, police officers, or public administrators with migrant parents, can also act as role models.

Yet, despite rising political awareness about the benefits of diversity in the public sector, youth with migrant parents remain underrepresented in public sector jobs in most countries, especially in longstanding European immigration destinations and in Southern Europe. The only exceptions are the United Kingdom, Australia and Norway, where native-born youth with immigrant parents are at equal shares as their peers with native-born parents (OECD/EU, 2018[1]).

Efforts to promote public sector employment among immigrants and their children have increased in several OECD countries over recent years. As a first and crucial step, remaining legal restrictions preventing foreign nationals from taking up public sector jobs have been lifted in most OECD countries since the beginning of the millennium. Several OECD countries have not only removed legal barriers, but actively promoted public sector recruitment of candidates with migrant parents – especially at the local and regional level. In Norway, the Anti-Discrimination Act outlines the obligation for government agencies to invite at least one applicant with migrant parents for an interview, provided the person is qualified for the position in question, a practice also implemented in a number of municipalities.

Austria, for example, has encouraged recruitment of applicants with migrant parents into the Viennese police force in the framework of the 'Vienna needs you' project. The initiative launched targeted information campaigns in co-operation with migrant communities, associations and schools. Finland offers targeted preparatory training, and professional education offers to encourage youth with migrant parents to start a teaching career. German cities and federal states aim to augment the share of public sector trainees with migrant parents through initiatives such as the 'Berlin needs you' and 'We are Hamburg' campaigns. Norway has gone a step further and introduced legal requirements for the public sector to invite a certain number of candidates with migrant parents for interviews. The country has also established diversity recruitment plans, set diversity targets and provides diversity training for recruitment staff in the public sector.

Table 7.1. Policies to promote participation of young people with migrant parents in the public sector in OECD countries, 2016

| | Programmes to promote participation in the public sector | |
	Yes/No	Instruments used
Australia	No	/
Austria	Yes (but not systematic)	*Wien braucht dich* (Vienna needs you): Pilot project by Viennese police to recruit applicants with migrant parents through Informing migrant communities with the help of the municipal department on integration and diversity (MA17) Kick-off and information events in migrant communities, associations and schools organised jointly by police and MA17 Tandem-Veranstaltungen (Polizei-MA17) in den Communities, Vereinen, Schulen
Belgium	Yes (but not systematic)	*Equal Opportunities and Diversity Plan*: Workforce diversity targets for cities in Flanders
Canada	Yes (not specific for public sector)	Short term work placements within participating public and private sector organisations for a specified period of time built on partnerships and it delivered with over 20 immigrant serving organisations in three locations across Canada
Chile	No (but pilot project for intercultural social mediators and mediation workshops in co-operation with migrant populations)	/
Czech Republic	No	/
Denmark	Yes	Equity benchmark for state and municipal governments (e.g. target setting; regular monitoring of employment statistics; small financial incentives)
Finland	Yes	*Specima projects* (2009-15): Preparatory training and continuing professional education for teaching occupations in various educational levels targeted at youth with migrant parents • Initiatives to increase the share of foreign language people in municipal administration • Specific recruitment initiatives for migrants from Somalia
Estonia		
France	No (but targeted recruitment of youth with social difficulties)	(Targeted recruitment of low-educated young people)
Germany	Yes	Advertisement encouraging migrant youth to apply for careers in the public sector
Greece	No	(no specific programmes)
Hungary	No	/
Iceland		
Israel		
Ireland	No	/
Italy	No	/
Japan		
Korea		
Latvia	No	/
Lithuania	n.a.	n.a.
Luxembourg	No	/
Mexico	No (except for migrant-specific programmes)	(*Community Leaders*: Young persons with migrant parents are recruited as 'community leaders" for a programme on prevention and care of unaccompanied children and adolescent migrants)
Netherlands	Yes (but not systematic)	*Amsterdam's Programma Diversiteit*: Setting workforce diversity targets
New Zealand	Not systematic	/
Norway	Yes	*Anti-Discrimination Act* Obligation for government agencies to invite at least one applicant with migrant parents for an interview, provided the person is qualified for the position in question (also implemented in a number of municipalities) Obligation for employers to make active, targeted and systematic efforts to promote

	Programmes to promote participation in the public sector	
	Yes/No	Instruments used
		equality and prevent discrimination in their undertakings and to report the equality measures that are/have been implemented Prohibition of direct and indirect discrimination on the basis of ethnicity, national origin, descent, skin colour, language, religion or belief
Poland	No	/
Portugal	Yes	*Choices Programme* (working groups "New Citizens" and "More Leaders") Reflexion about difficulties and problems that young new Portuguese citizens can face with their new citizenship Sessions in Democratic Institutions, Rights and Duties, Justice, Media and Global Citizenship for young adults from Cape Verde
Slovak Republic	No	/
Slovenia	No	/
Spain	No (but programs for all youth regardless of migrant parents)	/
Sweden	Yes	Affirmative action-type policies on ethnic and religious grounds
Switzerland	No	/
Turkey		
United Kingdom	Yes (but not specific for youth with migrant parents)	General affirmative action and employment equity policies
United States	Yes (but not specific for youth with migrant parents)	General affirmative action and employment equity policies

Note: n.a. = information not available.
Source: OECD questionnaire on the integration of young people with migrant parents 2016.

8. Facilitate the school-to-work transition

WHAT and WHY?

The transition from school to work is a critical point in the life of a young person. It can have long-term implications for future employment prospects, earnings and career trajectories (Scarpetta, Sonnet and Manfredi, 2010[81]). Youth with migrant parents – in particular those born abroad – are at a higher risk of not transitioning smoothly from education into the labour market and to find themselves neither in employment, education or training (Lillehagen and Birkelund, 2018[82]).

Part of the difficulties which youth with a migrant parents encounter are specific to those with a lower education level. These youth are also in many countries less likely to start and complete VET programmes (Jeon, 2019[83]). Yet, difficulties are also frequently observed among the highly educated, which indicates that differences in formal education cannot account for all of the observed differences (Connor et al., 2004[84]; Krause and Liebig, 2011[85]). Besides, young people with migrant parents and a higher education degree have a much harder time finding a position at their skill level than their peers of nativ-born descent (Crul, Keskiner and Lelie, 2017[86]).

One reason are social networks. Such networks are essential for job-search, especially for the very first contact with the labour market. They can provide information about job opportunities and tacit knowledge about the functioning of the labour market. Networks can further help to establish a first contact with an employer and may also improve the conditions for a person to apply and get accepted for a job. Children of immigrants tend to have fewer networks. They can generally rely on less assistance from their social network when searching for their first job than children of natives (McDonald, Lin and Ao, 2009[87]; Levitt, 2009[88]; Pedulla and Pager, 2019[89]). This is partly because their parents lack the relevant networks themselves, and parental support is often important for the first labour-market contact of youth. In addition, immigrant parents and their children often lack relevant knowledge about the functioning of the host-country labour market. Finally, there is the issue of discrimination (see next lesson).

WHO?

In OECD Europe, foreign-born youth who arrived as children are more likely to be not in education, employment or training (NEET) than their peers with native-born parents. In several OECD countries like Slovenia, Austria, Belgium, France and the Netherlands, their NEET-rates are twice as high. Differences are also observed for native-born youth with immigrant parents, though they tend to be less pronounced (OECD/EU, 2018[1]). While overall, NEET rates for youth with migrant parents are favourable in the OECD countries that were settled by immigration, there are important differences across origin countries. For example, those of Hispanic parentage show significant disadvantage in Canada and the United States United States (OECD, 2018[6]). . In the countries that were settled by immigration, young migrants born abroad – especially those with refugee parents – tend to be the focus group, whereas in OECD Europe, the programmes also include native-born youth with migrant parents.

Figure 8.1. Percentage of youth aged 15-34 who are not in employment, education or training (NEET), 2017

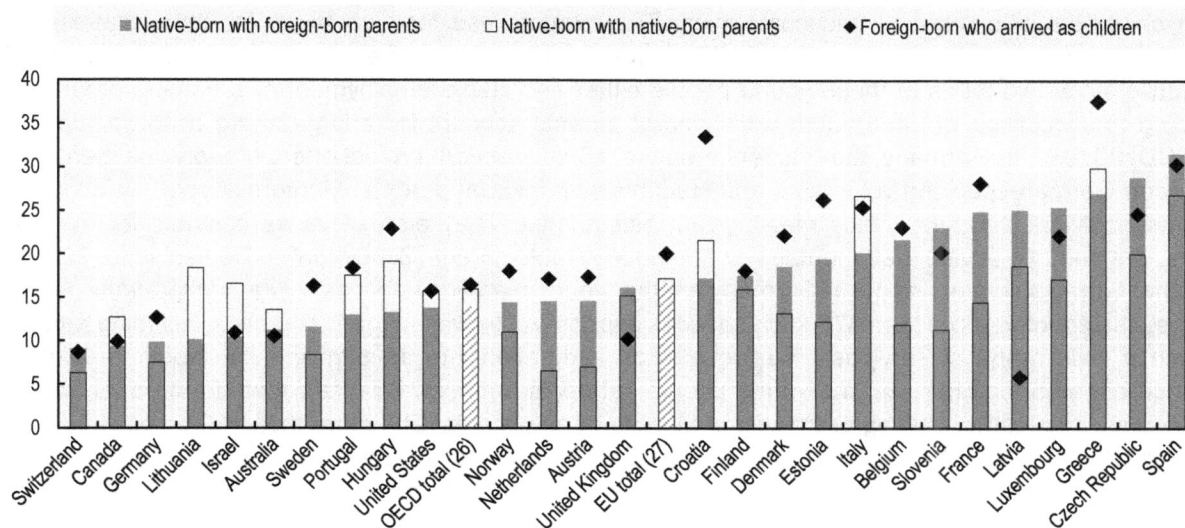

Source: OECD/EU (2018[1]).

HOW?

Policies to facilitate the school-to-work transition of youth with migrant parents include:

- Offering remedy for insufficient networks and lack of knowledge about the host-country labour market and its functioning, through targeted employment services or mentoring schemes
- Ensuring that financial barriers are not an obstacle to pursue internships
- Promoting participation and completion of vocational education and training (VET) programmes

Employment services that assist youth with migrant parents in their search for a first job can remedy for lack of relevant parental contacts and information about job opportunities. They aim to get youth in touch with potential employers and accompany them during the job-search period. Support offers include, for example, coaching, career guidance and assistance with CV and interview preparation.

In Australia, the 'Pathways to Employment Program' assists 12 to 25-year-old youth with migrant parents to bring their skills and experience to the workplace. It offers direct guidance, employment opportunities, traineeships, apprenticeships, and work experience across a wide range of industries. The programme also includes a mentorship scheme that matches volunteers with professional work experience with tertiary-level students. New Zealand supports the school-to-work transition of migrant students through various pathway programmes, including the vocational pathway programme linking student's knowledge and skills to job options. The "gateway" programme provide workplace experience along with relevant training, introducing students' to the wider industry training programme. Refugee students receive specific and individualised support through the Refugee Pathways and Career Planning programme in targeted high schools. In Finland, the youth guarantee scheme combines employment and education elements. The scheme guarantees a job or training placement within three months of becoming unemployed as well as a spot in upper secondary school, vocational education and training, apprenticeship training, or in a youth workshop for all school-leavers. Young immigrants can combine vocational upper secondary education and training with instruction of Finnish or Swedish as a second language or complete the entire training in their mother tongue. France has a large-scale mentoring programme with voluntary mentors – either business executives or newly retired people – who mentor a young person in a personal relationship over a number of months. These mentoring networks operate within a structure, most often a local mission (a body jointly financed by the French authorities and cities to facilitate youth employment), in partnership with chambers of commerce and companies. The mentors use their contacts, facilitate relations with companies and re-motivate young people. This programme, which has existed since 1993, is particularly effective since two-thirds of these young people either find stable employment or a training programme leading to a qualification, and youth with migrant parents account for a large share of the participants (OECD, 2010[5]). In Germany, the "student mentors" (*Schülerpaten*) project offers one-on-one mentorship between German-speaking volunteers and students with migrant parents. Mentors support students with their schoolwork through weekly meetings in their homes. They also serve as contacts for everyday questions and can advise their mentees on finding a suitable career (Schülerpaten Deutschland, 2021[90]). Another large-scale programme in Germany are the "youth migration services" (*Jugendmigrationsdienste*). Across the country, more than 470 such services support youth with migrant parents – including refugees – with a wide range of services. The focus is on integration into training and the labour market, via counsellors who together with the young people set goals and look for offers that fit individual abilities, provide job application training or training in the use of new media. The more than 950 employees reach around 120 000 young people every year. The initiative includes an online advisory service (jmd4you) free of charge and available in different languages (German Federal Ministry for Family, Seniors, Women and Youth, 2021[91]).

Financial barriers can represent a major additional hurdle that complicates pathways into meaningful employment for many children of immigrants. A case in point are internships, which – often unpaid or poorly paid – have become increasingly important to increase young people's employability in competitive sectors and establish professional networks. The programme 'Schotstek', run by the city of Hamburg, Germany, aims to overcome this barrier. The scheme provides excellent students from immigrant families with a close-knit and high-end professional network of entrepreneurs, founders of start-ups, scientists, artists, managers, politicians and other outstanding personalities, as well as a growing community of successful alumni. At the centre of the programme are individual coaching and mentoring activities, measures to improve the youngsters' networking and self-organisation skills, and projects aimed at broadening their horizons. The programme also provides financial support and assists with the search for internship opportunities and a first job. Provinces and Territories in Canada also provide grants and funding for youth apprenticeships. One example is the 'Ontario Youth Apprenticeship Program', a school-to-work transition programme at secondary schools. Therein full-time students in grades 11 and 12 earn co-operative education credits through work placements in skilled trades. While not specifically targeted at youth with migrant parents, they account for a significant proportion of participants.

Apprenticeships or vocational education and training (VET) programmes can facilitate the school-to-work transition. Policies can support youth with migrant parents to benefit more from such programmes. The first step is to have a sufficient number of training places available, the second is to raise awareness about and promote participation in vocational pathways among youth with migrant parents and including their parents (see Jeon (2019[83]) for an overview).

Switzerland and Germany, two OECD countries with wide-spread and renowned apprenticeship and vocational education and training systems, encourage the participation of youth with migrant parents in VET options through targeted schemes. In Switzerland, a 12-months apprenticeship preparation programme for young refugees provides up to 3 600 apprenticeship-preparation opportunities since 2018-21. Depending on participants' skills, the programme either provides early language training to integrate into skills development programmes, or language and professional training for vocational training. The programme targets future employment in sectors where there is a demand for skilled labour, such as health professions. Germany has a longstanding programme of 'regional vocational qualification networks' (*Berufliche QualifizierungsNetzwerke-BQNs*) across the country to promote access to vocational training, with a focus on youth with migrant parents. It includes information campaigns in schools (in regions with low initial educational attainment), acquisition of internships and vocational training spots for youth with migrant parents (in regions with limited vocational training places), and awareness-building among local employers and the general public. The progamme benefits from a co-operation of employment agencies, chambers of commerce, migrant organisations and local governments and entrepreneurs. The network connects youth with migrant parents and mainstream services. Germany has also a broad range of other activities to support youth with migrant parents in the VET system (see OECD (2019[92]) for an in-depth discussion).

9. Tackle discrimination and encourage diversity

WHAT and WHY?

Discrimination plays an important role in the persistent disadvantage faced by many youth with migrant parents. It has two distinct facets: individuals' subjective perception of being discriminated against and actual discrimination, for example in the hiring process. Regarding the latter, applicants with a 'a 'foreign-sounding name' often have to send twice as many applications before receiving a positive reply as their peers with otherwise similar CV but a "native-born" sounding name (Heath, Liebig and Simon, 2013[93]). EU-wide, almost one in five youth with immigrant parents feels part of a group that is discriminated against; significant shares of self-reported discrimination are also found in other OECD countries, including Canada, Israel and the United States. In Europe, the share is higher among those whose parents are native-born than among their foreign-born peers (OECD/EU, 2018[1]). While this does obviously not mean that the actual incidence is higher for the former group, it does point to a higher awareness of the issue.

Many individuals experience different forms of discrimination simultaneously based on their parental migration background, gender and gender identity, socio-economic status, and other aspects. These are not necessarily linked to a migration experience and immigrant parents. To tackle discrimination of youth with migrant parents effectively, intersectionality, the combination of individuals' several social and political identities needs to be taken into account, as policy impact can differ across otherwise similar groups with migrant parents (Richardson, Mittelmeier and Rienties, 2020[71]; Arai, Bursell and Nekby, 2016[94]).

However, not all disadvantage faced by youth with migrant parents is outright discrimination. Channels and practices through which companies or the public administration recruit and promote staff can also put youth with migrant parents at an inherent disadvantage. These more underlying, structural obstacles are addressed through diversity policies. Encouraging diversity means more than meeting targets in recruitment. Companies and the public sector must put in place effective diversity management and build a culture of inclusion to ensure that youth with migrant parents have equal opportunities (OECD, 2020[95]).

WHO?

Among young people born to immigrants in EU countries, almost one in five feels part of a group that is discriminated against on the grounds of ethnicity, nationality or race. One in seven report to experience discrimination because of their ethnicity, culture, race, or colour in Canada. In the United States, one native-born with immigrant parents in ten reports to have experienced discrimination in the workplace. In the United States, young men with migrant parents are more likely than their female peers to consider themselves part of a discriminated group. In the EU-countries, there is no gender difference. In many countries, those who are highly educated and those whose first language is not the language in their residing country report higher levels of discrimination (OECD/EU, 2018[1]).

Figure 9.1. Self-reported discrimination

Percentages, 15 to 34 year olds, 2008 16

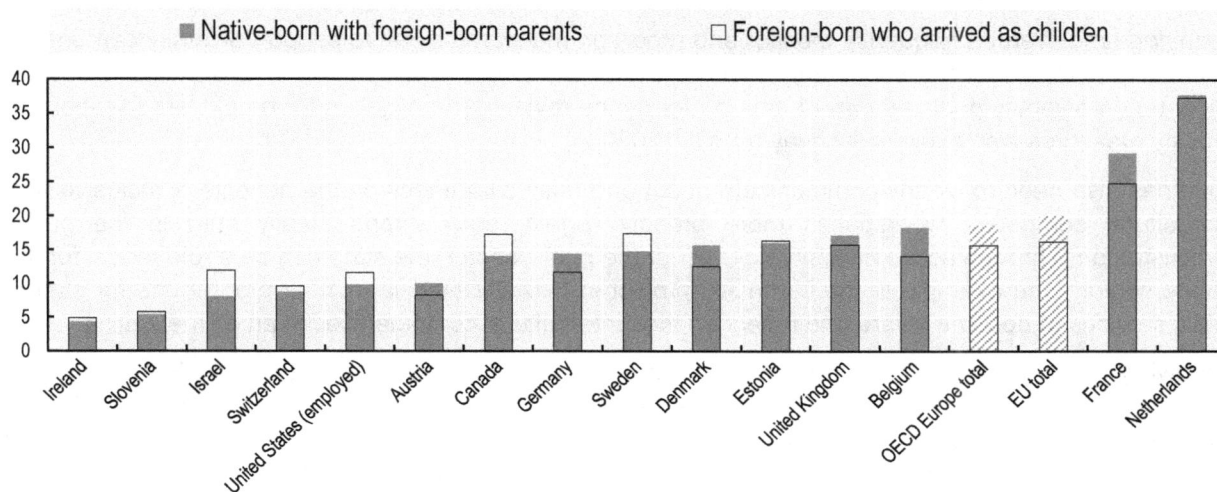

Source: OECD/EU (2018[1]).

HOW?

Stakeholders have a range of options available, including:

- Combating discriminatory hiring practises through legislation and ensuring equality of opportunity in recruitment
- Raising awareness about workplace rights and protection of all staff as well as about inclusive workplaces more broadly
- Assisting employers in achieving and sustaining a diverse workforce

Most OECD countries have taken measures to combat discriminatory hiring practices. However, the scale and scope of the steps vary widely. The most common action to combat discrimination are legal remedies. Many OECD countries have, for example, implemented non-discrimination legislation along with agencies responsible for monitoring its application. In the OECD countries that were settled by migration, like Australia, Canada and the United States, such legislation dates back several decades. In the European context, significant impetus came from the EU's Racial Equality Directive 2000/43/EC. The directive implemented the principle of equal treatment between persons irrespective of racial or ethnic origin.

Several OECD countries have also implemented more proactive policies to remove barriers that hamper access to the labour market for youth with migrant parents and promote professional upward mobility. Often they are based on targets, although hard quotas are rare. Countries like Finland, France, Germany and Norway, for example, have experimented with anonymous CVs, though generally only in small pilots. These tools, if carefully designed and monitored, can be effective in tackling discriminatory hiring practices (Heath, Liebig and Simon, 2013[93]).

Equality of opportunity in recruitment also includes to set up diverse selection teams and interview panels. It involves strengthening recourse and support mechanisms for potential victims of discrimination. This can also include setting up internal staff networks that promote diversity and inclusion (OECD, 2020[95]).

Along with anti-discrimination legislation, initiatives inform youth with migrant parents about workplace rights and protection and help them enforce these rights in cases where they are not respected. Australia, for example, has developed a "pay and conditions tool" to assist migrants and temporary visa holders in checking their salary and entitlements. The tool includes videos, brochures and posters informing about workplace rights in various languages. Moreover, it has put in place a free translator service for access to the Fair Work Ombudsman. Many other OECD countries undertook similar efforts.

Requiring employers to frequently monitor and report on measures taken to support diversity can ensure that rules and regulations are no 'empty shell' policy. In Sweden, for example, senior civil servants have to follow-up on diversity goals as part of their performance review. An obligation for employers to report on equality measures also exists in Norway (OECD, 2020[95]).

Countries also need to clearly communicate about and raise awareness on the benefits of inclusive and intercultural competent workspaces more broadly. Again, such efforts ideally start in the public administration. Through active diversity policies for the public sector, the state can be a role model for the private sector. One example is the Mana Aki project in New Zealand, a training programme for staff in public services to become aware and reflect on their intercultural competencies in an online setting.

A growing number of OECD countries have developed diversity labels or charters, to highlight diverse recruitment practices and to support the implementation of inclusion policies in companies. While not exclusively targeted at youth with migrant parents, they are often an important target group of such diversity tools, particularly in countries with large populations of youth with migrant parents and persistent disadvantage, such as in many longstanding European destinations. The French government, for example, provides companies with the possibility of passing an audit as to whether or not they use fair hiring and promotion practices. If enterprises satisfy six criteria, they can obtain a diversity label ('label diversité'). The criteria include a formal commitment to diversity; an active role of the social partners; equitable human resource procedures; communication by the enterprise on the question of diversity; concrete public measures in favour of diversity; and evaluation of practices. Along similar lines, Belgium grants specific diversity awards to employers with diversity-friendly company structures. Canada helps employers to obtain a diversified workforce by providing diversity training and support in developing inclusive hiring practices and retaining newcomers. Other OECD countries, including Austria, Belgium, Finland, Germany, Italy, the Netherlands, Spain and Sweden, have promoted 'diversity charters'. Signatories commit themselves to pro-diversity recruitment and career management practices.

Large corporations often find it easier to implement diversity-led recruitment practices and inclusion policies than small and medium-sized enterprises. SMEs have fewer resources, and recruitment channels are often subject to the bias of personal networks. To address this, in Flanders, SME employers could request financial support from the Flemish Department of Work and Social Economy to develop "Diversity Plans" until 2016. To support staff in their efforts to establish a diversity policy in their company trade unions deploy "diversity consultants" (van de Voorde and de Bruijn, 2010[96]). An organisation from France that seeks to equip employers with opportunities to recruit, retain and promote ethnically diverse staff is Mozaïk RH. The recruitment agency specialises at fostering diversity at the workplace by matching young candidates with migrant parents with local businesses. As part of its efforts, Mozaïk RH runs a job preparation programme, 'Mozaïk Campus', offering workshops, individual coaching and media-trainings. In Germany, the 'WelKMU' project targets highly educated youth with migrant parents to foster the presence of graduates with migrant parents in small and medium-sized enterprises (SMEs). WelKMU supports students in tertiary education through counselling, information sessions at universities and application workshops. The project also offers networking events, company fairs and company visits. SMEs receive short information videos and diversity training as well as targeted placement, counselling, trouble-shooting and mediation services from recruitment through the employment stage.

Table 9.1. Measures to tackle discriminatory hiring practices against young people with migrant parents in OECD countries, 2016

	Yes/No	Instruments used
Australia	Yes (but not all are specific to immigrants)	• Equal opportunity and non-discrimination laws • Initiatives to better inform migrants and temporary visa holders of their workplace rights and protections, including: • Pay And Conditions Tool (calculate.fairwork.gov.au) to assist workers check their salary and entitlements • The Fair Work Ombudsman's free interpreter service (13 14 50) with material in 27 languages • Videos in 14 different languages (posted on YouTube), workplace rights presentations and seminars with relevant groups, distribution of posters and brochures to migrant resource centres and community groups, pro-active engagement with ethnic media
Austria	Yes (but not targeted exclusively at young people with migrant parents)	• General Equal Treatment Act forbidding discrimination in the Federal Civil Service on ethnic grounds • Diversity charters for companies
Belgium	Yes	Development and use of diversity charters, diversity labels (in Brussels capital region) and specific diversity awards for employers
Canada	Yes	• Services helping employers meet the challenges of a diversified workforce and understand the business case of hiring internationally trained immigrants including diversity training, support in developing inclusive hiring practices and retaining newcomers • Support of Immigrant Employment Councils (IECs) through multi-stakeholder collaboration enhancing immigrant labour market integration, including by connecting skilled newcomers with Canadian employers • Canadian Human Rights Act and Canadian Employment Equity Act
Chile	No	/
Czech Republic	No	/
Denmark	Yes	Law against discrimination (SAMEN Act)
Estonia		
Finland	Yes	Use of diversity charters in companies Pilots on anonymous CVs in the public Sector in Helsinki and Espoo
France	Yes (but not targeted exclusively at young people with migrant parents)	• Contracts between government and firms to improve diversity and equity (e.g. diversity charters and diversity labels) • Use of anonymous CVs
Germany	Yes (not yet systematic)	• Use of diversity charters in companies • Use of anonymous CVs in various federal states
Greece	Yes	• Several EU funded projects against discrimination related to employment • Informational and awareness-raising campaigns against racism and xenophobia in several fields, including working conditions and hiring practices planned • National law implementing the Equal Treatment Directive 2000/43/EU and the General Framework Directive 2000/78/EU and prohibiting discrimination on the grounds of i.a. racial or ethnic origin regarding employment and occupation; entitling victims of discrimination to seek legal protection and imposing administrative sanctions on employers who discriminate
Hungary	No	/
Iceland		
Israel		
Ireland	Yes	• Employment Equality Acts 1998 – 2015 • 'Integrated Workplaces: An Action Strategy To Support Integrated Workplaces' includes a range of initiatives to assist employers and trade unions to respond effectively to the potential and challenges of a culturally diverse workforce and to create integrated workplaces.

	Yes/No	Instruments used
Italy	Yes Use of diversity charters in companies	Different projects on diversity management (financed by the Ministry of Interior and developed by regions in co-operation with trade unions or by the National Anti-Discrimination Office (UNAR)
Japan	No	/
Korea		
Latvia	Yes	*Promoting diversity (non-discrimination)* programme to reduce employment and socio-economic inclusion barriers for people at risk of social exclusion and discrimination (humanitarian migrants are a target group), while raising awareness on non-discrimination by providing motivation measures, support through social workers and mentors
Lithuania	No	/
Luxembourg	Yes	Use of diversity charters in companies
Mexico	Yes	*National Council to Prevent Discrimination* to promote and guarantee equality and non-discrimination rights via a *National Program for Equality and Non-Discrimination 2014-18* (includes a strategy on measures to reduce inequality in economic rights for discriminated people or groups and the protection of migrants and decent work inclusion opportunities)
Netherlands	Yes	Use of diversity charters in companies
New Zealand	No (not systematic)	/
Norway	No (not systematic in the private sector but some companies have programmes)	• The Federation of Norwegian Enterprises runs a leadership and boardroom competence development programme (*Global Future*) for multi-cultural talents with potential and ambition for professional advancement • Use of anonymous CVs • Anti-discrimination Act for public sector employment
Poland	No	/
Portugal	Yes	• Administrative complaint procedure for cases of racial discrimination run by a Commission for Equality and Against Racial Discrimination (CICDR) that is chaired by the High Commissioner for Migration and includes representatives elected by the parliament, representatives of employer associations, trade unions, immigrants and associations, NGOs and civil society. • Rising awareness about available legal and administrative remedies via a website (www.cicdr.pt) informing about legislation, legal documents, final administrative convictions, activities developed and the complaint procedure • Workshops and training sessions with technicians from the "Choices Programme", local mediators and young adults on the fight against racial discrimination
Slovak Republic	No	/
Slovenia	No	/
Spain	Yes	• Programmes at school to detect racism and xenophobic attitudes and sensitise students to prevent discrimination • Use of diversity charters in companies
Sweden	Yes	• Use of diversity charters in companies • Discrimination act • Ombudsman
Switzerland	Yes (part of cantonal integration programme)	Varies across cantons and employers (e.g. diversity management)
Turkey	Yes	Eligibility to same placement services and vocational training, career advice and rights related to work and social security than nationals
United Kingdom	Yes	•Equality and Human Right Commission •Equal Opportunities Policies
United States	Yes (not specific to immigrants)	•Title VII of the Civil Rights Act •Equal Employment Opportunity Act

Note: n.a. = information not available; / = not applicable.
Source: OECD questionnaire on the integration of young people with migrant parents 2016.

10. Foster social integration through sports and associations

WHAT and WHY?

Integration of youth with migrant parents is more than the elimination of performance gaps vis-à-vis youth of native-born parentage. It also goes beyond equal opportunities in education and employment. Successful integration also means to be full and equal part of the society. This can take various forms, including social, political, artistic or physical activities.

Participation in associations such as sports clubs, music groups or charities, provides an excellent opportunity for all youth to interact. As a training ground for civic skills and an arena for political recruitment, involvement in associations lowers the threshold for political participation, as data from Sweden suggest (Myrberg, 2010[97]). Active participation in associations also promotes opportunities to demonstrate talent and assume leadership roles in ways that might not be feasible in other settings (Makarova and Herzog, 2014[98]). Finally, it can provide the relevant networks for better inclusion in the labour market (McDonald, Spaaij and Dukic, 2018[99]).

Sport programmes, in particular, can attract marginalised young people without attaching the stigma usually associated with social intervention programmes (European Commission, 2016[100]). Despite these advantages, barriers for the participation of youth with migrant parents in associations exist. Such obstacles include costs, discrimination experience and a lack of sensitivity in training or gathering environments. Besides, youth with migrant parents, and in particular recent arrivals, can lack knowledge of mainstream sports and association services and might have inadequate access to transport (Block and Gibbs, 2017[101]).

Finally, pro-social engagement can also limit discrimination against immigrants, as it is taken as a signal for social integration. In a fictitious job application study, non-volunteering native-born candidates received more than twice as many job interview invitations as non-volunteering migrants. However, no unequal treatment was found between native-born and migrants when they revealed volunteering activities (Baert and Vujić, 2016[102]).

WHO?

Different stakeholders, including both governmental and non-governmental, and at all levels of government, can initiate efforts to involve youth of migrant parentage into sports and associations. Sport governing bodies or umbrella associations obviously have to implement the programmes though governmental institutions may support these with funding. Sports clubs and associations often reach out directly to youth with migrant parents, without specific national programmes. Schools and local community organisations are important intermediaries in this respect. They often partner with clubs and local authorities to attract young people with migrant parents into their environments.

HOW?

Public policies can set the framework to support and incentivise associations to play an important role in the integration process. This includes the following: Alongside setting incentives for associations, policies can counter barriers and obstacles for youth with immigrant parents:

- Reducing barriers to participate in associations through active reach-out, better information sharing and facilitated access through intermediaries like schools
- Increasing intercultural competences within associations to create more inclusive environments via special trainings and awareness-raising campaigns
- Supporting and showcasing successful projects that enhance the interaction between youth of native- and foreign-born parentage and facilitate entrance into the labour market

Better information about and access to associations and sports clubs for children of immigrants often involves partnerships among various stakeholders. The Football Association of Ireland, for example, has set up a nationwide after-school programme in partnership with schools and grass-root clubs. It links students with migrant parents and their parents to local sports clubs. The 6-week My-Club after-school programme is provided free of charge in primary schools with a high share of migrant students. Qualified coaches animate the sessions and offer interested migrant parents the opportunity to be trained as potential volunteer coaches along the way. At the end of the programme, students and volunteer parents are invited to visit and join their local sports club in the framework of a follow-up open day. In Denmark, the Get2Sport initiative supports sports clubs to reach and engage youth in sports association in areas with high concentrations of immigrants. Refugees, for example, are invited in co-operation with the local refugee centres and municipalities. The project provides a key link between the local sports clubs and the Danish Sport Confederation (DIF), which co-operates with the Danish Ministry of Immigration and Integration on this initiative (DIF, 2020[103]). The Italian Ministry of Labour's "Sport and Integration" project co-operates with the Italian Olympics Committee (CONI), to foster social integration and fight racial discrimination and intolerance. The ministry also supports awareness campaigns at schools and universities, where young people with migrant parents share their own experience on being part of sport associations. Italy is also piloting specific courses on "integration through sport" at five universities and provides school grants for young people with migrant parents to become sport teachers (Italian Ministry of Labour and Social Policies, 2020[104]).

Promoting inclusion and intercultural openness within associations and sports clubs entails various elements. One way is to provide intercultural trainings to coaches and club officials. The Italian Football Federation, for example, required representatives of all professional clubs to complete an awareness training with the Italian Sports Association (UISP). The European Sport Inclusion Network (ESPIN) promotes equal access of migrants and minorities to organised associations, amongst others by volunteering options for migrants and organising inclusion workshops for mainstream sports clubs and associations. Another example focusing on the inclusion of refugees is ASPIRE (Activity, Sport and Play for the Inclusion of Refugees in Europe), a collaborative project of nine European countries (ASPIRE, 2020[105]). The project has developed a training module that teaches facilitators of national and regional sport umbrella organisations to adapt existing coaching activities to the specific needs of refugees and migrants.

Participation in sports and associations can allow youth to acquire new knowledge and skills more generally. Learning options beneficial to youth with migrant parents can be language support linked to daily activities, use of educational concepts that foster social and inter-personal skills, and forms of civic engagement that allow youth to train leadership skills, irrespective of membership, for example as group workers or trainers. The German Olympic Sports Federation (DOSB), for instance, equips grass-root sports clubs financially and with qualification measures to provide targeted, low-threshold support to youth with migrant parents. As part of the DOSB's nationwide 'Integration Through Sports' (IdS) programme, support includes homework assistance, language training, assistance with visits at public authorities and job-search in more than 4 000 clubs across the country. The share of individuals with migrant parents at participating sports clubs was found to be roughly six times higher than the national average (DOSB, 2015[106]). In Portugal, the Art and Hope PARTIS initiative of the Calouste Gulbenkian Foundation supports projects that showcase the role of art in integrating vulnerable communities. From 2014-18, 33 projects created spaces for freedom and learning, aiming to overcome prejudices and nurturing mutual respect and understanding between groups and communities that would not normally cross paths. More recently, a further 15 projects have been selected through an open tender between 2019 and 2021 (Calouste Gulbenkian Foundation, 2020[107]). The Workers Educational Association of Sweden lists a number of good practises for community engagement in their online handbook "methods" (Workers Educational Association of Sweden, 2020[108]). One such example is the engagement of native- and non-native speakers in a choir. Singing together enhances participants' Swedish skills by practicing the pronunciation and creates a space to interact with each other and exchange. Participants are also invited to perform non-Swedish pieces on local stages and events which, in turn, creates awareness in Sweden about immigrants' and their children's cultural heritage.

Countries can also encourage national governing bodies of sport and volunteering organisations to reach minimum targets for equal participation. The United Kingdom, for instance, has introduced an equality standard back in 2004 that evaluates sports clubs on their openness to groups under-represented in sport and makes support dependent upon this evaluation.

Associations can provide links to the labour market. In Denmark, the project "From the Bench to the Pitch" was created in 2002 by one of the largest football clubs in Denmark, Brøndby IF, in co-operation with the Municipality of Brøndby and the Ministry of Integration. The aim of the project is to establish contacts between young people with migrant parents and the club's network of sponsor firms. The club thereby acts as an intermediary. The project is also open to young people who are not part of the club. The advantage of using the club as an intermediary is that it has knowledge about the strengths' and weaknesses of the young people involved, while at the same time having access to company representatives who have taken a commitment to support the club and its activities. In Chile, the foundation "Music for Integration" facilitates contact among persons with and without migrant parents, but also enables musicians to teach their instruments to children, allowing for a diverse role modelling to youngsters and a skills training in this teaching role among instructors (Música para la Integración, 2020[109]).

Finally, some countries and municipalities award special prices for projects and associations with particularly high integration efforts and successes. The integration price for sports in Austria and the integration price in Lower Bavaria, for example, recognise the integration efforts of the winning associations or projects (Sportunion Austria, 2020[110]).

11. Encourage naturalisation

WHAT and WHY?

Citizenship is a powerful asset that can positively impact various aspects of life. Acquiring citizenship legally enables full social and civic participation and also builds a sense of belonging (Hainmueller, Hangartner and Pietrantuono, 2017[111]; Bloemraad, 2006[112]; OECD, 2011[113]).

What is more, citizenship is associated with better labour market outcomes for youth with migrant parents. As nationals, children of immigrants are more likely to work in high-skilled jobs and the public sector than their peers with foreign nationality. The citizenship premium can play a vital role when youth start to look for a job, as youth who are nationals receive more invitations to job interviews. Reasons include perceived lower administrative costs to hire a national, as opposed to a foreigner, as well as positive signalling of skills and broader social integration (OECD, 2011[113]). Finally, holding host country nationality facilitates access to financial resources. Advantages include access to scholarships and credits, enabling youth with migrant parents to start or expand business ideas.

In spite of all these advantages, many youth with migrant parents who would be eligible for host-country citizenship do not take it up.

WHO?

The share of native-born children of immigrants holding the nationality of their country of residence varies widely across OECD countries. Much of this variation reflects differences in legislation for birthright citizenship. In countries, where the principle of birthright citizenship (jus soli) applies, such as in Canada and the United States, native-born children of immigrants have automatic citizenship. The same is essentially true for countries with a modified version of jus soli like France and the United Kingdom. In other countries, native-born youth can naturalise easily. In Sweden and the Netherlands, more than 90% of the native-born children of immigrants aged 20-29 are nationals. In contrast, in countries where citizenship descends based on parents' nationality (jus sanguinis), like Austria and Switzerland, shares of native-born children of immigrants nationality are lowest (OECD, 2011[113]).

HOW?

Countries have a range of policy tools at their disposal to encourage citizenship take-up among children of immigrants. Among the most common measures are the following set of actions:

- Ensuring that native-born youth and those raised in the country access citizenship easily, by creating birthright entitlements for native-born and facilitated pathways for others
- Allowing for dual citizenship
- Promoting citizenship take-up by disseminating information about naturalisation and the favourable impact it can have on life

The most straightforward way to ensure that native-born children of immigrants become nationals is to automatically attribute nationality at birth to those born in the country. This jus soli principle is prevalent in the OECD countries settled by migration. However, recently, a number of European OECD countries made amendments to their citizenship laws to facilitate access to citizenship among native-born children of immigrants. Almost half of all OECD countries have integrated elements of jus soli into their citizenship legislation. Often, however, birthright citizenship in Europe is conditional upon a parent having resided for a specified period in the country. In countries where nationality is still largely transferred via descent (i.e. jus sanguinis), regulations can be more or less stringent. Minimum residence requirements for regular naturalisation range from three to ten years with an average of five years. Applicants often need to prove a certain level of language proficiency, knowledge of institutions and civic values, self-sufficiency, and a clear criminal record.

In the vast majority of countries, native-born children of immigrants enjoy certain facilitations, including shorter residency requirements, exemptions from tests or other obligations, and an entitlement to declare citizenship at a certain age. Typically, the option to declare citizenship exists only within a specified time window following legal age. However, in a few countries, children (or parents on their behalf) may declare citizenship earlier. In Sweden, for example, children (or their legal guardian) may declare citizenship after three years of residence. In Greece and Portugal, this option exists at the start or upon completion of primary school. Australia and Luxembourg automatically attribute nationality to children born and raised in their country who are not eligible to birthright citizenship at age 10 and 18, respectively.

Enabling youth with migrant parents to keep other nationalities is a critical way to encourage citizenship take-up. Indeed, for many youth, the cost associated with giving up the nationality of a parent constitutes a significant obstacle. In the past, several countries have required children of immigrants to choose one nationality. The rationale behind such policies were fears that dual and multiple citizenship might decrease loyalty to the country of residence and lead to abuse of rights. However, it is increasingly recognised that such fears are unwarranted and dual citizenship is now recognised in more than three-quarters of OECD countries. In some countries, this possibility is subject to conditions. For instance, in Germany, since 2014, children of immigrants who have been growing up in the country can maintain dual nationality. As a precondition, they must have lived in Germany for eight years, when turning 21 and have attended a German school for six years or completed vocational training. Previously, such youth were obliged to choose one citizenship upon becoming 18 until the age of 23.

Public information campaigns to promote naturalisation among eligible immigrant groups can help to increase citizenship take-up. Such programmes typically explain the required steps to naturalise, as well as the benefits of holding citizenship. Countries settled by migration have made such efforts for many years, in line with a longstanding perception of newly arrived immigrants as future citizens.

Canada, the OECD country with the highest citizenship take-up rate, has a long tradition of encouraging and facilitating naturalisation among permanent residents. An example is the 'Citizenship Awareness Program', an initiative of the federal government, with support of provinces and local communities. The programme includes the distribution of the citizenship study guide 'Discover Canada', the organisation of an annual citizenship week, and social media campaigns for promoting citizenship. Initiatives to reach immigrant youth include emails to school principals to use citizenship material and school visits of citizenship judges, who are expected to conduct outreach activities one half-day per month. According to a survey-based evaluation of the programme, activities that reinforced feelings of belonging and permanency facilitated naturalisation (Government of Canada, 2014[114]).

In the United States, the National Partnership for New Americans (NPNA) co-operates with community partners, mayor's offices, members of congress, and labour unions to co-ordinate the nationwide nonpartisan 'Naturalise NOW' campaign. Through application assistance events, communication, outreach, and co-ordinated policy strategies, the campaign encourages eligible lawful permanent residents to naturalise.

High fees for naturalisation might hinder youth from naturalising. In many countries, fees are negligible, though not everywhere. In an attempt to address this barrier, a range of countries have lowered fees or introduced fee waivers. In the United Kingdom, for example, the 'Citizenship Payment Plan' supports families to cover the cost of their children's citizenship application fees. The programme includes legal support to immigrant families, a one-off loan to the family to cover the high cost of a citizenship application, as well as a 12-month repayment plan. In the United States, the use of partial fee waivers as well as credit card fee payments to raise naturalisation rates among low-income immigrants have been tried. An example is the 'NaturalizNY' initiative, a public-private partnership. The programme, which uses a lottery to offer immigrants in the state of New York a voucher, is covering the naturalisation application fee of USD 725. An evaluation of the policy intervention suggests that those who were offered a voucher were twice as likely to apply as those who had to cover the fee themselves (Hainmueller et al., 2018[115]).

Table 11.1. National legislation on the acquisition of citizenship at birth for children of immigrants and legal framework with respect to dual citizenship, 2018

	Adoption of (elements of) jus soli	Legal framework with respect to dual citizenship
Australia	Yes	Yes
Austria	No	Yes (children who have obtained dual nationality by birth/origin may maintain dual citizenship, also beyond the age of 18, according to Austrian law)
Belgium	Yes (if at least one parent was also born in Belgium and has lived in Belgium during at least 5 of the 10 years preceding the child`s birth)	Yes
Canada	Yes	Yes
Chile	Yes (if at least one parent resides in Chile at the time of the child`s birth)	Yes
Czech Republic	No	Yes
Denmark	No	Yes (if dual nationality was obtained at birth and in some cases of naturalisation)
Estonia	No	No
Finland	Yes (if the child's parents have refugee status or have been granted protection against the authorities of their country of nationality)	Yes
France	Yes (if at least one parent was also born in France)	Yes
Germany	Yes (if at least one parent resided in Germany for at least 8 years prior to the child's birth)	Yes
Greece	No	Yes
Hungary	No	Yes
Iceland	No	Yes
Israel	No	Yes (for Jewish persons)
Ireland	Yes (if at least one parent resided for a minimum of 3 out of 4 years in Ireland prior to the child`s birth)	Yes
Italy	No	Yes
Japan	Yes　(if born in Japan and both of the parents are unknown or are without nationality.)	No
Korea	No	Yes
Latvia	No	No (except in exceptional cases for naturalising foreigners of certain nationalities and Latvians abroad)
Lithuania	No	Yes (children who have obtained dual nationality by birth may maintain both citizenships, also beyond the age of 21, according to Lithuanian law)
Luxembourg	Yes (if at least one parent was also born in Luxembourg)	Yes
Mexico	Yes	Yes
Netherlands	Yes (if at least one parent was also born in the	No (except in exceptional cases)

	Adoption of (elements of) jus soli	Legal framework with respect to dual citizenship
	Netherlands)	
New Zealand	Yes (if at least one parent is a permanent resident)	Yes
Norway	No	No (except in exceptional cases)
Poland	No	Yes
Portugal	Yes (if at least one parent was either born in Portugal or has been resident for at least 5 years prior to the child's birth)	Yes
Slovak Republic	No	Yes
Slovenia	No	No (except in exceptional cases)
Spain	Yes (if at least one parent was also born in Spain)	No
Sweden	Yes	Yes
Switzerland	No	Yes
Turkey	No	Yes
United Kingdom	Yes (if at least one parent was settled in the UK at the time of the child's birth)	Yes
United States	Yes	Yes

Note: n.a. = information not available; / = not applicable. This table does not account for cases where a new-born child would become stateless or is found in the territory of unknown identity.
Source: National provisions based on publicly available information, compiled by the OECD Secretariat, 2018.

Table 11.2. Legal framework with respect to the conditions for the acquisition of citizenship through naturalisation in OECD countries, 2018

	Standard residency requirement	Facilitations for children born or raised in the country
Australia	4 years	Yes (minors are exempt from citizenship test; children born to foreign nationals who are not permanent residents become citizens automatically at age 10)
Austria	10 years (6 years if exceptionally well-integrated)	No
Belgium	5 or 10 years	Yes (youth who were born in Belgium can claim citizenship between age 18 and 30 or their parents, if they have resided in Belgium for at least 10 years, can file the claim before the child's 12th birthday)
Canada	5 years of which 3 physically present	Yes (youth under 18 years of age are exempt from meeting the language and knowledge requirement and, under certain conditions, the residence requirement)
Chile	5 years	Yes (youth born in Chile to foreign non-resident parents may declare Chilean nationality by option within one year of their 18th birthday)
Czech Republic	5 years permanent residence or 10 years total	Yes (youth educated in the Czech Republic are exempt from language and citizenship test; young adults (18-21) resident since age 10 are eligible to a rights-based "declaration" procedure)
Denmark	9 years	Yes (children born and raised in Denmark are, under certain conditions, entitled to Danish citizenship by a declaration submitted before the age of 19)
Estonia	8 years	Yes (young immigrants who have lived in Estonia for eight years and descendants of emigrants)
Finland	5 years (4 years for fluent Finnish or Swedish speakers)	Yes (children raised in Finland can claim citizenship between age 18 and 22)
France	5 years	Yes (children who were born in France and have lived at least 5 consecutive years in France after their 8th birthday are entitled to citizenship)
Germany	8 years (6 years in exceptional cases)	Yes (youth who have obtained a German school leaving diploma are exempt from passing the citizenship test)
Greece	7 years	Yes (minors whose parents resided for a minimum of 5 years in Greece prior to the child's birth can declare Greek citizenship when entering primary education, as well as those who have attended nine years of compulsory education or have graduated from a Greek

	Standard residency requirement	Facilitations for children born or raised in the country
		university or technical college in the past three years)
Hungary	8 years	Yes, a non-Hungarian citizen who has resided in Hungary continuously for a period of five years prior, may be naturalised on preferential terms if born or residing in Hungary before reaching legal age, and if other conditions are satisfied. The criteria of continuous residence in Hungary, may be waived for minors, who applied together with their parents or if their parent(s) were granted Hungarian citizenship. Yes, a refugee recognised by the Hungarian authority or a stateless person may be naturalised if resided continuously in Hungary for 3 years prior.
Iceland	7 years	Yes (18-or-19-year-old youth resident since age 11 can declare themselves citizens)
Israel	Permanent residence for 3 out of 5 years preceding the application	n.a.
Ireland	5 years	No
Italy	10 years	No
Japan	5 years	Yes for persons born in Japan, and continuously having a domicile or residence in Japan for three years or more or whose father or mother (excluding an adoptive parent) was born in Japan. Yes for persons without any nationality since the time of birth, and continuously having a domicile in Japan for three years or more since that time
Korea	5 years	No
Latvia	5 years	No (except stateless/non-citizen children born after independence who can be registered by their parents as Latvian citizens)
Lithuania	10 years	No
Luxembourg	5 years	Yes (youth who lived in Luxembourg between age 13 and 18 and whose parents resided in Luxembourg before the child was born automatically obtain nationality at age 18)
Mexico	5 years	n.a.
Netherlands	7 years	Yes (children born or raised in the Netherlands can claim citizenship at age 18, before age 18 they face no or a reduced residence requirement)
New Zealand	5 years	Yes (children under 16 years of age may be exempted from requirements)
Norway	7 years	Yes (children below the age of 12, born or raised in the country face shorter residence requirements; those aged 12+ go through the same procedure as newcomer immigrants)
Poland	8 years (1 year for people of Polish origin)	No
Portugal	6 years	Yes (children born in the country are entitled to citizenship after their first cycle of compulsory education; foreign-born children must naturalise with or after their parents)
Slovak Republic	8 years	No
Slovenia	10 years	Yes (children born or raised in Slovenia and youth who completed higher education in Slovenia face shorter actual residence requirements)
Spain	10 years	Yes (for children born in Spain the residency requirement is reduced to 1 year)
Sweden	5 years	Yes (children of immigrants are eligible to citizenship after 3 years of residence in the country upon notification by their parents)
Switzerland	10 years	Yes (years spent in Switzerland between the ages of eight and 18 count double towards the residence requirement; youth who were born and educated in Switzerland and whose family lives in Switzerland in the third generation are eligible for a facilitated procedure)
Turkey	5 years	No
United Kingdom	5 years	Yes (minors who were born in the UK and either spent their first 10 years there or whose parents received permanent residence can register as citizens)
United States	5 years	n.a.

Note: n.a. = information not available; / = not applicable. The minimum residence duration displayed in this table does not account for specific cases, such as for the spouses of nationals, who often face shorter residence requirements.
Source: National provisions based on publicly available information, compiled by the OECD Secretariat, 2018.

References

Akgündüz, Y. and S. Heijnen (2018), "Impact of Funding Targeted Pre-school Interventions on School Readiness: Evidence from the Netherlands", *De Economist*, Vol. 166/2, pp. 155-178, http://dx.doi.org/10.1007/s10645-018-9314-2. [24]

Antony-Newman, M. (2018), "Parental involvement of immigrant parents: a meta-synthesis", *Educational Review*, Vol. 71/3, pp. 362-381, http://dx.doi.org/10.1080/00131911.2017.1423278. [39]

Arai, M., M. Bursell and L. Nekby (2016), "The Reverse Gender Gap in Ethnic Discrimination: Employer Stereotypes of Men and Women with Arabic Names,", *International Migration Review*, Vol. 50/2, pp. 385-412, http://dx.doi.org/10.1111/imre.12170. [94]

ASPIRE (2020), *ASPIRE - Activity, Sport and Play for the Inclusion of Refugees in Europe |ASPIRE*, http://www.aspiresport.eu/index.php/blog/aspire-activity-sport-and-play-inclusion-refugees-europe (accessed on 3 September 2020). [105]

Aydemir, A., W. Chen and M. Corak (2013), "Intergenerational Education Mobility among the Children of Canadian Immigrants", *Canadian Public Policy*, Vol. 39/Supplement 1, pp. S107-S122, http://dx.doi.org/10.3138/cpp.39.supplement1.s107. [69]

Baert, S. and S. Vujić (2016), "Immigrant volunteering: A way out of labour market discrimination?", *Economics Letters*, Vol. 146, pp. 95-98, http://dx.doi.org/10.1016/j.econlet.2016.07.035. [102]

Balladares, J. and M. Kankaraš (2020), "Attendance in early childhood education and care programmes and academic proficiencies at age 15", *OECD Education Working Papers*, No. 214, OECD Publishing, Paris, https://dx.doi.org/10.1787/f16c7ae5-en. [16]

Becker, B. and C. Gresch (2016), "Bildungsaspirationen in Familien mit Migrationshintergrund", in *Ethnische Ungleichheiten im Bildungsverlauf*, Springer Fachmedien Wiesbaden, http://dx.doi.org/10.1007/978-3-658-04322-3_3. [41]

Behtoui, A. (2019), "Constructions of self-identification: children of immigrants in Sweden", *Identities*, pp. 1-20, http://dx.doi.org/10.1080/1070289x.2019.1658396. [9]

Bénabou, R., F. Kramarz and C. Prost (2009), "The French zones d'éducation prioritaire: Much ado about nothing?", *Economics of Education Review*, Vol. 28/3, pp. 345-356, http://dx.doi.org/10.1016/j.econedurev.2008.04.005. [54]

Benton, T. and K. White (2007), *Raising the Achievement of Bilingual Learners in Primary Schools: Statistical Analysis. Research Report DCSF-RR006*, http://131.211.208.19/login?auth=eng&url=http://ovidsp.ovid.com/ovidweb.cgi?T=JS&CSC=Y&NEWS=N&PAGE=fulltext&D=eric3&AN=ED502448 (accessed on 8 April 2020). [58]

Bergseng, B., E. Degler and S. Lüthi (2019), *Unlocking the Potential of Migrants in Germany*, OECD Reviews of Vocational Education and Training, OECD Publishing, Paris, https://dx.doi.org/10.1787/82ccc2a3-en. [92]

Beuchert, L., V. Christensen and S. Jensen (2020), *PISA Etnisk 2018. PISA 2018 med fokus på elever med indvandrerbaggrund.*, http://www.vive.dk/media/pure/15029/4184497. [46]

Block, K. and L. Gibbs (2017), "Promoting Social Inclusion through Sport for Refugee-Background Youth in Australia: Analysing Different Participation Models", *Social Inclusion*, Vol. 5/2, p. 91, http://dx.doi.org/10.17645/si.v5i2.903. [101]

Bloemraad, I. (2006), *Becoming a citizen : incorporating immigrants and refugees in the United States and Canada*, University of California Press. [112]

Boliver, V. (2013), "How fair is access to more prestigious UK universities?", *The British Journal of Sociology*, Vol. 64/2, pp. 344-364, http://dx.doi.org/10.1111/1468-4446.12021. [74]

Borgonovi, F. and G. Montt (2012), "Parental Involvement in Selected PISA Countries and Economies", *OECD Education Working Papers*, No. 73, OECD Publishing, Paris, https://dx.doi.org/10.1787/5k990rk0jsjj-en. [38]

Bratsberg, B., O. Raaum and K. Røed (2011), *Educating Children of Immigrants: Closing the Gap in Norwegian Schools*. [27]

Brunello, G. and M. De Paola (2017), *School segregation of immigrants and its effects on educational outcomes in Europe*, Prepared for the European Commission, European Expert Network on Economics of Education (EENEE). [49]

Buunk, A., J. Peiró and C. Griffioen (2007), "A Positive Role Model May Stimulate Career-Oriented Behavior", *Journal of Applied Social Psychology*, Vol. 37/7, pp. 1489-1500, http://dx.doi.org/10.1111/j.1559-1816.2007.00223.x. [78]

Calouste Gulbenkian Foundation (2020), *Art and Hope: PARTIS Initiative Trajectories 2014-2018*, https://gulbenkian.pt/en/publication/arte-comunidade-percursos-da-iniciativa-partis/. [107]

Camilleri, A. et al. (2013), *Evolving diversity II: Participation of students with an immigrant background in European higher education*, MENON Network, Brussels, Belgium. [72]

Canton of Zurich (2017), *Volksschule. Qualität in multikulturellen Schulen (QUIMS). Berichterstattung 2014–2016 und Massnahmen 2018–2022*, http://www.zh.ch/de/bildungsdirektion/generalsekretariat-der-bildungsdirektion/bildungsrat/suche-bildungsratsbeschluesse/2017-brb-25-volksschule-qualitaet-in-multikulturellen-schulen-quims.html#906829797. [51]

Chmielewski, A. (2014), "An International Comparison of Achievement Inequality in Within- and Between-School Tracking Systems", *American Journal of Education*, Vol. 120/3, pp. 293-324, http://dx.doi.org/10.1086/675529. [33]

Collins, K. and R. Clément (2012), "Language and Prejudice: Direct and Moderated Effects", *Journal of Language and Social Psychology*, http://dx.doi.org/10.1177/0261927X12446611. [10]

Connor, H. et al. (2004), *Why the difference? A closer look at higher education minority ethnic students and graduates*, Institute for Employment Studies. [84]

Covarrubias, R. and S. Fryberg (2015), "The impact of self-relevant representations on school belonging for Native American students.", *Cultural Diversity and Ethnic Minority Psychology*, Vol. 21/1, pp. 10-18, http://dx.doi.org/10.1037/a0037819. [79]

Crul, M., E. Keskiner and F. Lelie (2017), "The upcoming new elite among children of immigrants: a cross-country and cross-sector comparison", *Ethnic and Racial Studies*, Vol. 40/2, pp. 209-229, http://dx.doi.org/10.1080/01419870.2017.1245432. [86]

Crul, M. and H. Vermeulen (2003), "The Second Generation in Europe", *International Migration Review*, Vol. 37/4, pp. 965-986, http://dx.doi.org/10.1111/j.1747-7379.2003.tb00166.x. [31]

Damm, A. et al. (2020), *Effects of Busing on Test Scores and the Wellbeing of Bilingual Pupils: Resources Matter*, Aarhus University. [47]

De Witte, K. et al. (2013), "The Impact of Institutional Context, Education and Labour Market Policies on Early School Leaving: A comparative analysis of EU countries", *European Journal of Education*, Vol. 48/3, pp. 331-345, http://dx.doi.org/10.1111/ejed.12034. [60]

DIF (2020), *DIF | Get2Sport*, http://dx.doi.org/www.dif.dk/da/get2sport (accessed on 27 July 2020). [103]

DOSB, D. (2015), *Der Artikel-und Informationsdienst des Deutschen Olympischen Sportbundes DOSB-PRESSE*, http://www.dosb.de (accessed on 20 April 2020). [106]

Drange, N. and K. Telle (2015), "Promoting integration of immigrants: Effects of free child care on child enrollment and parental employment", *Labour Economics*, Vol. 34, pp. 26-38, http://dx.doi.org/10.1016/j.labeco.2015.03.006. [23]

European Commission (2016), *Mapping of good practices relating to social inclusion of migrants through sport*, https://op.europa.eu/en/publication-detail/-/publication/f1174f30-7975-11e6-b076-01aa75ed71a1 (accessed on 20 April 2020). [100]

European Commission (2014), *Preventing early school leaving in Europe. Lessons learned from second chance education.*, https://op.europa.eu/en/publication-detail/-/publication/575dc3dc-a6fb-4701-94a2-b53d62704567 (accessed on 28 July 2020). [64]

European Commission (2013), *Reducing early school leaving: Key messages and policy support Final Report of the Thematic Working Group on Early School Leaving*, https://ec.europa.eu/education/sites/education/files/early-school-leaving-group2013-report_en.pdf. [62]

European Commission, EACEA and Eurydice (2016), *Structural Indicators on Early Childhood Education and Care in Europe – 2016. Eurydice Report.*, http://dx.doi.org/10.2797/78330. [26]

Fachkommission Integrationsfähigkeit (2021), *Gemeinsam die Einwanderungsgesellschaft gestalten. Bericht der Fachkommission der Bundesregierung zu den Rahmenbedingungen der Integrationsfähigkeit.*, https://www.fachkommission-integrationsfaehigkeit.de/fk-int/dokumente (accessed on 23 February 2021). [13]

German Federal Ministry for Family, Seniors, Women and Youth (2021), *Jugendmigrationsdienste*, https://www.bmfsfj.de/bmfsfj/themen/kinder-und-jugend/integration-und-chancen-fuer-junge-menschen/jugendmigrationsdienste/jugendmigrationsdienste-86208. [91]

German Federal Ministry for Family, Seniors, Women and Youth (2021), *Stark im Beruf - Ziele und Zahlen*, https://www.starkimberuf.de/programm/ziele-und-zahlen. [44]

Godwin, R. et al. (2006), "Sinking Swann: Public School Choice and the Resegregation of Charlotte's Public Schools", *Review of Policy Research*, Vol. 23/5, pp. 983-997, http://dx.doi.org/10.1111/j.1541-1338.2006.00246.x. [48]

Government of British Columbia, P. (2018), *Words Matter - Guidelines on Using Inclusive Language in the Workplace*. [12]

Government of Canada (2014), *Evaluation of the Citizenship Awareness Program*, https://www.canada.ca/en/immigration-refugees-citizenship/corporate/reports-statistics/evaluations/citizenship-awareness-program/summary.html.   [114]

Hadjar, A. and J. Scharf (2018), "The value of education among immigrants and non-immigrants and how this translates into educational aspirations: a comparison of four European countries", *Journal of Ethnic and Migration Studies*, Vol. 45/5, pp. 711-734, http://dx.doi.org/10.1080/1369183x.2018.1433025.   [42]

Hagelskamp, C., C. Suárez-Orozco and D. Hughes (2010), "Migrating to Opportunities: How Family Migration Motivations Shape Academic Trajectories among Newcomer Immigrant Youth", *Journal of Social Issues*, Vol. 66/4, pp. 717-739, http://dx.doi.org/10.1111/j.1540-4560.2010.01672.x.   [40]

Hainmueller, J., D. Hangartner and G. Pietrantuono (2017), "Catalyst or crown: Does naturalization promote the long-term social integration of immigrants?", *American Political Science Review*, Vol. 111/2, pp. 256-276, http://dx.doi.org/10.1017/S0003055416000745.   [111]

Hainmueller, J. et al. (2018), "A randomized controlled design reveals barriers to citizenship for low-income immigrants", *Proceedings of the National Academy of Sciences*, Vol. 115/5, pp. 939-944, http://dx.doi.org/10.1073/pnas.1714254115.   [115]

Hanushek, E., J. Kain and S. Rivkin (2001), *Why Public Schools Lose Teachers*, National Bureau of Economic Research, Cambridge, MA, http://dx.doi.org/10.3386/w8599.   [55]

Hanushek, E., S. Rivkin and J. Schiman (2016), "Dynamic effects of teacher turnover on the quality of instruction", *Economics of Education Review*, Vol. 55, pp. 132-148, http://dx.doi.org/10.1016/j.econedurev.2016.08.004.   [53]

Heath, A. and E. Kilpi-Jakonen (2012), "Immigrant Children's Age at Arrival and Assessment Results", *OECD Education Working Papers*, No. 75, OECD Publishing, Paris, https://dx.doi.org/10.1787/5k993zsz6g7h-en.   [29]

Heath, A., T. Liebig and P. Simon (2013), *Discrimination against immigrants – measurement, incidence and policy instruments*, OECD Publishing, Paris, https://dx.doi.org/10.1787/migr_outlook-2013-en.   [93]

Heckman, J. (2006), "Skill Formation and the Economics of Investing in Disadvantaged Children", *Science*, Vol. 312/5782, pp. 1900-1902, http://dx.doi.org/10.1126/science.1128898.   [21]

Hermansen, A. (2017), "Age at Arrival and Life Chances Among Childhood Immigrants", *Demography*, Vol. 54/1, pp. 201-229, http://dx.doi.org/10.1007/s13524-016-0535-1.   [28]

Italian Ministry of Labour and Social Policies (2020), *Promozione delle Politiche di Integrazione attraverso lo Sport*, http://www.integrazionemigranti.gov.it/Progetti-e-azioni/Pagine/Sport-Integrazione.aspx.   [104]

Jeon, S. (2019), *Unlocking the Potential of Migrants: Cross-country Analysis*, OECD Reviews of Vocational Education and Training, OECD Publishing, Paris, https://dx.doi.org/10.1787/045be9b0-en.   [83]

Joblinge Foundation (2018), *Annual Report and Impact Report 2018*, http://www.joblinge.de/fileadmin/user_upload/English/Joblinge-Jahresbericht-2018-eng.pdf (accessed on 28 July 2020).   [66]

Karsten, S. (2006), "Policies for disadvantaged children under scrutiny: the Dutch policy compared with policies in France, England, Flanders and the USA", *Comparative Education*, Vol. 42/2, pp. 261-282, http://dx.doi.org/10.1080/03050060600628694. [36]

Karunanayake, D. and M. Nauta (2004), "The Relationship Between Race and Students' Identified Career Role Models and Perceived Role Model Influence", *The Career Development Quarterly*, Vol. 52/3, pp. 225-234, http://dx.doi.org/10.1002/j.2161-0045.2004.tb00644.x. [76]

Kim, Y., S. Mok and T. Seidel (2020), *Parental influences on immigrant students' achievement-related motivation and achievement: A meta-analysis*, Elsevier Ltd, http://dx.doi.org/10.1016/j.edurev.2020.100327. [43]

Krause, K. and T. Liebig (2011), "The Labour Market Integration of Immigrants and their Children in Austria", *OECD Social, Employment and Migration Working Papers*, No. 127, OECD Publishing, Paris, https://dx.doi.org/10.1787/5kg264fz6p8w-en. [85]

Kristen, C., D. Reimer and I. Kogan (2008), "Higher Education Entry of Turkish Immigrant Youth in Germany", *International Journal of Comparative Sociology*, Vol. 49/2-3, pp 127-151, http://dx.doi.org/10.1177/0020715208088909. [70]

Leseman, P. et al. (2017), "Effectiveness of Dutch targeted preschool education policy for disadvantaged children.", in Blossfeld, H. et al. (eds.), *Childcare, early education, and social inequality – An international perspective*, Edward Elgar, Celtenham, UK. [25]

Levitt, P. (2009), "Roots and routes: Understanding the lives of the second generation transnationally", *Journal of Ethnic and Migration Studies*, Vol. 35/7, pp. 1225-1242, http://dx.doi.org/10.1080/13691830903006309. [88]

Lillehagen, M. and G. Birkelund (2018), *Ethnic inequalities in the transition from education to work: A longitudinal analysis of school, college and university graduates*, Center for Open Science, http://dx.doi.org/10.31235/osf.io/4ew53. [82]

Lyche, C. (2010), "Taking on the Completion Challenge: A Literature Review on Policies to Prevent Dropout and Early School Leaving", *OECD Education Working Papers*, No. 53, OECD Publishing, Paris, https://dx.doi.org/10.1787/5km4m2t59cmr-en. [59]

Makarova, E. and W. Herzog (2014), "Sport as a means of immigrant youth integration: an empirical study of sports, intercultural relations, and immigrant youth integration in Switzerland", *Sportwissenschaft*, Vol. 44/1, pp. 1-9, http://dx.doi.org/10.1007/s12662-013-0321-9. [98]

McDonald, B., R. Spaaij and D. Dukic (2018), "Moments of social inclusion: asylum seekers, football and solidarity", *Sport in Society*, Vol. 22/6, pp. 935-949, http://dx.doi.org/10.1080/17430437.2018.1504774. [99]

McDonald, S., N. Lin and D. Ao (2009), "Networks of opportunity: Gender, race, and job leads", *Social Problems*, Vol. 56/3, pp. 385-402, http://dx.doi.org/10.1525/sp.2009.56.3.385. [87]

Música para la Integración (2020), *Music for refugee integration in Chile*, https://globalcompactrefugees.org/article/music-refugee-integration-chile (accessed on 13 January 2021). [109]

Myrberg, G. (2010), "Political Integration through Associational Affiliation? Immigrants and Native Swedes in Greater Stockholm", *Journal of Ethnic and Migration Studies*, Vol. 37/1, pp. 99-115, http://dx.doi.org/10.1080/1369183x.2011.521366. [97]

Neidell, M. and J. Waldfogel (2009), "Program participation of immigrant children: Evidence from the local availability of Head Start", *Economics of Education Review*, Vol. 28/6, pp. 704-715, http://dx.doi.org/10.1016/j.econedurev.2009.06.004. [19]

Nouwen, W., N. Clycq and D. Uličná (2015), *Reducing the Risk that Youth with a Migrant Background in Europe Will Leave School Early | migrationpolicy.org*, http://www.migrationpolicy.org/research/reducing-risk-youth-migrant-background-europe-will-leave-school-early (accessed on 28 July 2020). [61]

Nusche, D. (2009), "What Works in Migrant Education?: A Review of Evidence and Policy Options", *OECD Education Working Papers*, No. 22, OECD Publishing, Paris, https://dx.doi.org/10.1787/227131784531. [35]

Oakes, J. (2005), *Keeping track: How schools structure inequality*, Yale University Press. [32]

OECD (2020), *All Hands In? Making Diversity Work for All*, OECD Publishing, Paris, https://dx.doi.org/10.1787/efb14583-en. [95]

OECD (2019), *OECD Skills Strategy Flanders: Assessment and Recommendations*, OECD Skills Studies, OECD Publishing, Paris, https://dx.doi.org/10.1787/9789264309791-en. [67]

OECD (2018), *Catching Up? Country Studies on Intergenerational Mobility and Children of Immigrants*, OECD Publishing, Paris, https://dx.doi.org/10.1787/9789264301030-en. [6]

OECD (2018), *Effective Teacher Policies: Insights from PISA*, PISA, OECD Publishing, Paris, https://dx.doi.org/10.1787/9789264301603-en. [52]

OECD (2018), *The Resilience of Students with an Immigrant Background: Factors that Shape Well-being*, OECD Reviews of Migrant Education, OECD Publishing, Paris, https://dx.doi.org/10.1787/9789264292093-en. [2]

OECD (2017), *Catching Up? Intergenerational Mobility and Children of Immigrants*, OECD Publishing, Paris, https://dx.doi.org/10.1787/9789264288041-en. [3]

OECD (2017), *Employment and Skills Strategies in Slovenia*, OECD Reviews on Local Job Creation, OECD Publishing, Paris, https://dx.doi.org/10.1787/9789264278929-en. [65]

OECD (2017), *Making Integration Work: Family Migrants*, Making Integration Work, OECD Publishing, Paris, https://dx.doi.org/10.1787/9789264279520-en. [30]

OECD (2017), *Starting Strong 2017: Key OECD Indicators on Early Childhood Education and Care*, Starting Strong, OECD Publishing, Paris, https://dx.doi.org/10.1787/9789264276116-en. [18]

OECD (2016), *Working Together: Skills and Labour Market Integration of Immigrants and their Children in Sweden*, OECD Publishing, Paris, https://dx.doi.org/10.1787/9789264257382-en. [68]

OECD (2015), *Immigrant Students at School: Easing the Journey towards Integration*, OECD Reviews of Migrant Education, OECD Publishing, Paris, https://dx.doi.org/10.1787/9789264249509-en. [17]

OECD (2014), *International Migration Outlook 2014*, OECD Publishing, Paris, https://dx.doi.org/10.1787/migr_outlook-2014-en. [20]

OECD (2013), "Discrimination against immigrants – measurement, incidence and policy instruments", in *International Migration Outlook 2013*, OECD Publishing, Paris, https://dx.doi.org/10.1787/migr_outlook-2013-7-en. [116]

OECD (2012), *Equity and Quality in Education: Supporting Disadvantaged Students and Schools*, OECD Publishing, Paris, https://dx.doi.org/10.1787/9789264130852-en. [56]

OECD (2011), *Naturalisation: A Passport for the Better Integration of Immigrants?*, OECD Publishing, Paris, https://dx.doi.org/10.1787/9789264099104-en. [113]

OECD (2010), *Equal opportunities? The Labour Market Integration of the Children of Immigrants.*, OECD. [80]

OECD (2010), *Equal Opportunities?: The Labour Market Integration of the Children of Immigrants*, OECD Publishing, Paris, https://dx.doi.org/10.1787/9789264086395-en. [5]

OECD/EU (2018), *Settling In 2018: Indicators of Immigrant Integration*, OECD Publishing, Paris/European Union, Brussels, https://dx.doi.org/10.1787/9789264307216-en. [1]

OECD/EU (2015), *Indicators of Immigrant Integration 2015: Settling In*, OECD Publishing, Paris/European Union, Brussels, https://dx.doi.org/10.1787/9789264234024-en. [4]

Office of the United Nations High Commissioner for Human Rights (2018), *A Human Rights-Based Approach to Data. Leaving no one behind in the 2030 Agende for Sustainable Development*, https://www.ohchr.org/Documents/Issues/HRIndicators/GuidanceNoteonApproachtoData.pdf (accessed on 16 June 2020). [15]

Pedulla, D. and D. Pager (2019), "Race and Networks in the Job Search Process", *American Sociological Review*, Vol. 84/6, pp. 983-1012, http://dx.doi.org/10.1177/0003122419883255. [89]

Portes, A. and R. Rumbaut (2001), "Legacies: The story of the immigrant second generation", https://books.google.com/books?hl=fr&lr=&id=2hWsgN2P8gcC&oi=fnd&pg=PR9&ots=vHfrQaaHXy&sig=q4MsH_GvkqAtnVnqFpKbcYkCPig (accessed on 6 April 2020). [8]

Richardson, J., J. Mittelmeier and B. Rienties (2020), "The role of gender, social class and ethnicity in participation and academic attainment in UK higher education: an update", *Oxford Review of Education*, pp. 1-17, http://dx.doi.org/10.1080/03054985.2019.1702012. [71]

Roos, M. (2017), *Entwicklungen von 2014 bis 2016 im Programm QUIMS mit Fokus auf den obligatorischen Schwerpunkten*, Bericht im Auftrag des Volksschulamts des Kantons Zürich, http://wiki.edu-ict.zh.ch/_media/quims/roos_2017_quims_bericht_2014-16_def.pdf. [50]

Scarpetta, S., A. Sonnet and T. Manfredi (2010), "Rising Youth Unemployment During The Crisis: How to Prevent Negative Long-term Consequences on a Generation?", *OECD Social, Employment and Migration Working Papers*, No. 106, OECD Publishing, Paris, https://dx.doi.org/10.1787/5kmh79zb2mmv-en. [81]

Schleicher, A. (2014), *Equity, Excellence and Inclusiveness in Education: Policy Lessons from Around the World*, International Summit on the Teaching Profession, OECD Publishing, Paris, https://dx.doi.org/10.1787/9789264214033-en. [57]

Schneeweis, N. (2015), "Immigrant concentration in schools: Consequences for native and migrant students", *Labour Economics*, Vol. 35, pp. 63-76, http://dx.doi.org/10.1016/j.labeco.2015.03.004. [45]

Schülerpaten Deutschland (2021), *Hauptseite - Schülerpaten Deutschland*, https://schuelerpaten-deutschland.de/. [90]

Shiner, M. and P. Noden (2014), "'Why are you applying there?': 'race', class and the construction of higher education 'choice' in the United Kingdom", *British Journal of Sociology of Education*, Vol. 36/8, pp. 1170-1191, http://dx.doi.org/10.1080/01425692.2014.902299. [73]

Sportunion Austria (2020), *Integrationspreis Sport 2020 - SPORTUNION Österreich*, https://sportunion.at/news/2020/11/04/integrationspreis-sport-2020/?cli_action=1610549173.49 (accessed on 13 January 2021). [110]

Tasmanian Government, D. (2019), *Inclusive Language Guidelines*. [11]

The Netherlands Scientific Council for Government Policy (2017), *Migration and Classification: Towards a Multiple Migration Idiom*, https://english.wrr.nl/topics/migration-diversity/documents/investigation/2017/06/26/summary-migration-and-classification-towards-a-multiple-migration-idiom (accessed on 6 April 2020). [14]

UNICEF (2017), *STUDENTS AT RISK OF DROPPING OUT. Policy and Practice Pointers for Enrolling All Children and Adolescents in School and Preventing Dropout*, https://www.unicef.org/eca/reports/monitoring-education-participation (accessed on 8 April 2020). [63]

Valero, D., A. Keller and A. Hirschi (2019), "The Perceived Influence of Role Models and Early Career Development in Native and Migrant Youth", *Journal of Career Development*, Vol. 46/3, pp. 265-279, http://dx.doi.org/10.1177/0894845318763905. [75]

van de Voorde, M. and H. de Bruijn (2010), "Mainstreaming the Flemish Employment Equity and Diversity Policy", in *Equal Opportunities?: The Labour Market Integration of the Children of Immigrants*, OECD Publishing, Paris, https://dx.doi.org/10.1787/9789264086395-10-en. [96]

Wilder, S. (2013), "Effects of parental involvement on academic achievement: a meta-synthesis", *Educational Review*, Vol. 66/3, pp. 377-397, http://dx.doi.org/10.1080/00131911.2013.780009. [37]

Will, A. (2019), "The German statistical category "migration background": Historical roots, revisions and shortcomings", *Ethnicities*, Vol. 19/3, pp. 535-557, http://dx.doi.org/10.1177/1468796819833437. [7]

Wiśniewski, J. and M. Zahorska (2020), "Reforming education in Poland", in *Audacious Education Purposes: How Governments Transform the Goals of Education Systems*, Springer International Publishing, http://dx.doi.org/10.1007/978-3-030-41882-3_7. [34]

Woessmann, L. and G. Schuetz (2006), *Efficiency and Equity in European Education and Training Systems*, Prepared for the European Commission, European Expert Network on Economics of Education (EENEE). [22]

Workers Educational Association of Sweden (2020), *Methods – Exchange for empowerment*, http://methods.arbetarnasbildningsforbund.se/?lang=en (accessed on 13 January 2021). [108]

Zirkel, S. (2002), "Is There A Place for Me? Role Models and Academic Identity among White Students and Students of Color", *Teachers College Record*, Vol. 104/2, pp. 357-376, http://dx.doi.org/10.1111/1467-9620.00166.

[77]